INSTRUCTOR'S GUIDE TO THE

PROTECTION OFFICER TRAINING MANUAL

INSTRUCTOR'S GUIDE TO THE PROTECTION OFFICER TRAINING MANUAL

Fifth Edition

International Foundation for Protection Officers

7500 Macleod Trail South, Calgary, Alberta, Canada; Bellingham Business Park, 4200 Meridian, Bellingham, Washington, USA

Butterworth–Heinemann
Boston   London   Oxford   Singapore   Sydney   Toronto   Wellington

Copyright © 1992 by Butterworth–Heinemann, a division of Reed Publishing (USA) Inc. All rights reserved.

No part of this publication may be reproduced, stored in a retrieval system, or transmitted, in any form or by any means, electronic, mechanical, photocopying, recording, or otherwise, without the prior written permission of the publisher.

 Recognizing the important of preserving what has been written, it is the policy of Butterworth–Heinemann to have the books it publishes printed on acid-free paper, and we exert our best efforts to that end.

Library of Congress Cataloging-in-Publication Data
International Foundation for Protection Officers. Minion, Ronald R. ed.
    Protection Officer Training Manual/International Foundation for Protection Officers.
    p.   cm.
    ISBN 0–7506–9292–8 (alk. paper)
    1. Police, Private—Training of—United States—Handbooks, manuals, etc.
    2. Private Security services—United States—Handbooks, manuals, etc. I. International Foundation for Protection Officers.
    HV8291.U6P76   1992
    363.2'89'0683—dc20   91-41687
                                                                                   CIP

British Library Cataloguing in Publication Data
Minion, Ronald R. ed. International Foundation for Protection Officers.
    Protection Officer Training Manual.
    I. Title
    658.47

    ISBN 0–7506–9292–8

Butterworth–Heinemann
80 Montvale Avenue
Stoneham, MA 02180

10 9 8 7 6 5 4 3 2 1

Printed in the United States of America

CONTENTS

Part One

    Content Summary Review 1
    Objectives 11
    Organization of Program 11
    Study Resources 11
    Interim Assessment 11
    Final Examination 11
    Course Evaluation 12
    Review/Discussion Questions 12

Part Two

    On Site: Practical Training Exercises and Learning Objectives 22
    Final Study Suggestion 27
    CPO Interim Examination Questions 28
    Manual Quiz Answers 29

CONTENT SUMMARY REVIEW

PURPOSE AND SCOPE

For the convenience of readers of this manual, each unit and chapter has been summarized. An abbreviated narrative of the contents are set forth in a manner that offers a quick and concise reference to the core material.

There are 10 units, containing 27 regular chapters and one separate Miscellaneous Section. Pages are numbered by unit, chapter and page, i.e. Unit V, Chapter 2, Page 7 would appear:

PROTECTION OFFICER TRAINING MANUAL: Unit V - 2) - 7

The chapter on Learning Skills and Study Habits is essential for candidates wishing for maximum utilization of this manual as the C.P.O. Course Text.

Protection Officer Ethics

The Security Industry has not developed a recognized code of ethics or standard of conduct for Security Personnel. Senior Management in large corporations, both private and public, have often been remiss for failing to develop a code of ethics for all employees to be used as a guide to encourage integrity-based behavior.

Leaders must not only produce a code of ethics, but demonstrate by exemplary personal and business conduct that rules are for everyone in the organization. Because of the nature of the duties performed by protection officers, it is imperative that a code of ethics be readily available for constant reference and application to duties performed.

The matter of professional ethics for protection officers is a topic that is seldom discussed, but is of vital importance to the entire profession. These ethics provide not only a guide to the officer, but also for the various levels of security management and the user of security service.

Learning Skills & Study Habits

This chapter has been prepared by a professional educator with a view to enhance the opportunity for readers to better understand the contents of each section. While the Manual is primarily designed for the Certified Protection Officer (CPO) program, every member of the security community that reads this manual may improve their ability to retain information.

Educators have determined that by purely reading straight script, the retention rate varies, but can be improved by applying a number of effect learning techniques that are discussed in this chapter. Some effective study habits and methods of retaining the core information in each chapter are presented to readers to assist in gaining more of the valuable contents of this professional manual. Timely illustrations, charts, photos and other descriptive graphics and comparisons make this manual easy to read and understand.

UNIT I

History of Private Security

To fully understand the state of the Security Industry, one must examine the history of security. This chapter covering history begins by dealing with the security methods employed by tribal chiefs to enhance protection among members of the tribe, and will take the reader through the days of the Emperor of Rome, move through the middle ages and examine the present state of the industry.

Statistics are made available from the Hallcrest Report, prepared for the National Institute of Justice. This is a thoroughly researched chapter developed to provide a better understanding of the present state of the security industry, and how public law enforcement and justice administration interfaces with Private and Corporate Security.

There are a number of important trends surfacing in the security community such as a need for law enforcement to better utilize the resources available by involving security in crime prevention practises. Enlarged roles and more responsibility for security organizations in the overall protection process is anticipated.

Field Notes - Report Writing

This chapter begins by stressing the importance of the written word, particularly as it relates to the role of the protection officer. The notebook is described as a 'tool of the trade'. The reader is given guidance in selection of a suitable notebook, proper note-taking, notebook maintenance, notes for future reference, utilizing the notebook as an aid in giving evidence.

The best methods of transferring information from the notebook to the report format is discussed in detail. The importance of a well-written report is underscored as the most effective means by which the work of the protection officer may be evaluated by fellow officers, supervisors, the courts and other departments and organizations both private and public.

The chapter discusses the various kinds of reports that may be encountered by the protection officer and how these reports form an integral part of the security organization's administration process. Finally, the chapter spells out how the written report conveys to the reader how competent the officer really is in terms of effective task completion.

Memory & Observations

The modern Protection Officer must improve memory skills, as do Security Supervisors and Managers. This is a popular and useful chapter for all security personnel. What one professional protection officer might observe during a normal tour of duty after studying this chapter and one who had not, is quite different.

By using the methods of observation suggested in this chapter, readers will discover that there is an opportunity to detect, observe and report more information than previously thought possible.

This chapter will enhance the opportunity for the protection officer to be more resourceful, observant and provide more in-depth and meaningful reports. By combining learning skills, study habits and memory and observation techniques, a much higher level of information retention will result, as well as improved performance.

Preventive Security

The role of the modern Protection Officer is one of prevention. Prevention and security awareness are topics that are constantly referred to in this manual. Good prevention equals effective security and loss control. Security personnel must be ever-conscientious of the need for preventive security in the performance of security duties.

Generally, the police role is one of detection and apprehension, although law enforcement organizations make every effort to prevent crime. On the contrary, security officers must be aware of methods to prevent acts or omissions that will endanger the safety and security of people, assets and information of the organization that is protected.

Preventive security is an excellent lead-in chapter for readers to consider as reference is made to the many complex aspects of security work. This chapter provides an overview of preventive security philosophies and discusses management expectations in developing and maintaining sound security measures.

UNIT II

Patrol Techniques

The patrol function can be significantly improved by applying some of the awareness, observation, memory and preventive skills covered in Level One of this manual. This is one of the most important functions of the modern protection officer.

Results of effective patrolling can enhance the overall protection of personnel, assets and information. Protection officers are advised as to the kind of facility violations to be expected, a description of potential perpetrators and the danger signals that can alert the officer.

This chapter gives the reader information on patrol preparation, execution and reporting. It clearly illustrates the most effective methods of patrolling and provides excellent cautionary guidelines to promote officer safety. The importance of the connection between the patrol, field notes and the finished report is reiterated in this chapter.

Security - Safety Considerations

There has always been a close link between safety and security. For example, the title 'Public Safety Officer' frequently replaces a more traditional security-orientated rank description. And some organizations have attempted to incorporate a total 'Loss Control concept' by including safety, security and fire protection into one organizational job description.

The Protection Officer is in an ideal position to combine safety responsibilities with regular security duties. This chapter gives the reader a clear picture of the overall organizational safety structure, individual responsibilities and how the protection officer can bring safety hazards to light. By close scrutiny of potential safety risks and effective reporting, the protection officer can make beneficial contributions to organizational safety.

Traffic Control

Vehicular movement at every location that is protected by security becomes a responsibility of the Protection Officer. This chapter first discusses the need for proper preparation for duty by describing the physical items required to get the job done. The importance of a 'good attitude' is explained and the need for full officer attention to safety is emphasized.

Signs and automatic signals are discussed as well as careful description of hand gestures and the officer's position when directing traffic. The use of the whistle can maximize effective traffic movement and control. Reference is made to pedestrian traffic, handicapped persons, emergency vehicles and how the traffic officer can assist police in the execution of this important security function.

The chapter concludes by providing some useful tips on traffic control and site locations from which the protection officer may expect to perform traffic control duties.

Crowd Management

The effective management of large groups of people is becoming a major role of the Protection Officer. Failure to understand or execute correct procedures can lead to disastrous consequences. Effective crowd control is the difference between a smooth flow of pedestrian traffic and a hysterical mob of uncontrollable individuals who can cause serious injury or death to innocent people and countless amounts of property damage.

This chapter describes the kind of gatherings of people that can be defined as a crowd, demonstration, riot or a disaster. The reader is made to understand the causes of crowd formation such as casual, social, political or economic. It discusses countermeasures that can be employed to neutralize a crowd that is becoming unruly.

Manpower considerations are covered as well as liaison with local law enforcement personnel. Additional methods of crowd management such as isolating individuals, removing leaders, diverting attention and other effective tactics are covered in detail. The chapter concludes with a crowd control planning checklist and shows some illustrations that indicate effective personnel deployment.

Crime Scenes, Evidence Preservation

How successfully the Protection Officer is able to protect the crime scene and preserve evidence has considerable impact on the outcome of a criminal investigation either by the police or senior members of the security organization.

The protection officer who encounters a crime scene must first take measures that will afford officer safety. Criminal apprehension is less important than reducing the chance of injury or death to protection personnel.

Once it has been established that a crime has taken place and in fact a crime scene does exist, the officer must then seek backup personnel. The boundaries of the crime scene must be determined and declared a sterile area. No one without authorization from the senior security or police officials may be allowed into the restricted area.

The protection officer has specific responsibilities, foremost of which is properly prepared notes that may later be helpful in crime detection activities. This chapter explains what the protection officer might expect to find at a crime scene. It also provides information as to how the protection officer can best render assistance to investigating officers on the scene. The chapter concludes with a caution to the protection officer: "Don't touch - preserve and protect".

UNIT III

Physical Security

This facet of security is vitally important for the Protection Officer. Almost every facility requires various forms of physical security, from a simple access control system such as key control to the various sophisticated, integrated control access methods ranging from magnetic strip cards, voice prints, laser readers and new technology such as retina scan (eye readers). Advanced hi-tech access control systems,

Closed Circuit T.V., robots, alarm systems that monitor unauthorized and authorized movement of personnel, as well as the environment are becoming common methods designed to improve physical security.

At the top of the list of physical security measures is the trained protection officer. Adding integrated security systems to any facility means more effective deployment of security personnel. Personnel, hardware, software are all part of the protection link.

This chapter discusses physical security in-depth and it is essential that officers fully understand the connection between the human and technical aspects of physical security. This chapter discusses the five steps that are involved with physical security, namely:

Identification of Assets: Asset protection includes safeguarding personnel, information and all corporate possessions that can be classified and protected. Corporate Assets must be accurately inventoried so that effective measures of protection can be implemented to preserve these assets. Failure to develop and maintain productive asset protection can most certainly result in business failure.

Loss Events: Threats to organizational assets must be identified. The potential consequences of the threat, the likelihood of the loss event actually occurring and the effects that such a loss event would have on the organization is a vital exercise in physical security planning. The protection officer can be an integral part of the system that monitors the effectiveness of physical security measures.

Occurrence Probability: There are a number of methods that will assist in determining with reasonable accuracy, the likelihood of a loss event actually occuring. This condition has significant bearing on the level of physical security that must be placed upon assets that are affected. Gathering intelligence from past, present and anticipated events is a function that can be enhanced by effective officer observations and reports.

Impact of Occurrence: The effects that a loss event may have on an organization are critical in the overall loss control planning process. For example, a disaster, man-made or by act of God, could require numerous contingency plans ranging from auxiliary power to such considerations as mutual aid from other corporations. When a loss event occurs, the protection officer is often first on the scene and must take immediate remedial action.

Countermeasures: There are a wide range of countermeasures that must be considered in the physical security planning process. Asset identification, potential loss events, the probability of an occurrence and the impact this occurrence (event) would have on the organization are all factors that influence the level of physical security. Readers should relate Emergency, Disaster Planning techniques covered separately in level four of this manual when considering physical security countermeasures.

General Physical Security Considerations

This chapter goes on to explain the various lines of defence that are incorporated into the physical security process. The **first line of defence** is the property boundary that requires a varying degree of security that is based on many factors such as location, natural barriers, assets protected and the kind of pedestrian or vehicular traffic expected.

The **second line of defence** is the exterior of the building that can be secured in a number of effective manners. If physical security planning was incorporated into the building design, less add-on measures are required. However, older buildings require special measures applied to the walls, doors, windows, skylights and other areas of possible access.

The **final line of defence** is the interior of the building. Security to areas such as the computer centre, boardroom, safes, vaults and other offices must be considered as well as the location and role of employees, the value of assets and the classification of proprietary information.

There are a number of vital considerations in security that are discussed in detail. The chapter goes on to discuss lighting, glazing, intrusion detection and devices, sensors, control systems, security monitoring, card access, locking hardware, CCTV, safes and vaults, fire-resistant containers and fencing.

With the advent of high technology in the administration of physical security, we sometimes tend to lose sight of the 'old lock and key'. There is a danger that in planning for effective security controls, we have a tendency to sometimes 'overkill' in the implementation of security control systems.

At most Security Exhibitions, usually held in conjunction with security seminars or conferences, there are often 75-80% of the exhibits displaying various kinds of access control systems. Less attention is paid to such traditional devices like effective key control systems.

The old theory that identifies what is critical to the survival of the organization and how vulnerable to compromise these assets may be is still a prime consideration in physical security planning. We must not lose sight of the human aspect of hi-tech security. For, without well-trained, alert officers providing back-up and support to security systems, they become virtually useless. Personnel is a key component to any integrated security system.

UNIT IV

Explosive Devices, Bomb Threat & Search Procedure

This chapter begins by pointing out that explosives are not that difficult to obtain and are commonly used by the construction industry and certain other professions. The use of bombs and other explosive devices are not exclusive to terrorists and threats are often received from disgruntled employees, individuals with political motives and even pranksters. Explosives can be acquired by theft, legal purchase, mail order in some instances, and of course there are home mixtures. Numerous publications are available that provide explicit instruction on the production and use of explosive devices.

Because of the mounting threat of terrorism in our society, the countless incidents of bombings and threats, the Protection Officer must be conversant with this ever-increasing problem. This chapter provides excellent information that will assist the protection officer by understanding relevant terminology and the use and deployment of explosive devices. The following topics are covered, supported by excellent graphics:

- Bombs
- Bomb Threats
- Explosives
- Bomb Incident Plans
- Blasting Caps
- Pyrotechnics
- Explosive Ordnance Disposal
- Bombers

Explosive firing systems are described. The explosion results from a chain reaction of specific elements in an explosive fire system. There are two types: electric and non-electric. Basic components of the firing system are illustrated throughout this chapter. However, protection officers should take every possible step to expand their knowledge of the items used in a firing system. There are several different types of activating sources, firing lines, detonators and explosives.

Bombs are basically an explosive firing system in a box or other container. While this seems like a simple description, readers are cautioned that there is no such thing as a simple bomb.

Bombs can be found concealed in such conveyances as a shoe box, briefcase, backpacks and such items as appliances, lunch boxes, thermos bottles, books or even ink pens can be coverted into hazardous devices. These are sometimes referred to as booby-traps. Bombs are activated in many ways such as:

- Chemical Reaction
- Motional
- Mechanical
- Frictional
- Electrical

This chapter cites a number of Do's and Don'ts such as **don't** cut wires, handle, etc. **Do** report, evacuate and isolate area. And if time permits, attend to such details as opening doors, windows and removing flammables from the immediate area.

The chapter provides much detail with respect to first officer on the scene actions that are necessary for effective execution of bomb threat procedures. The chapter goes on to describe hazardous devices, domestic explosives and other items termed "nasty devices". Preventive measures are discussed in detail.

The chapter goes into considerable detail discussing bomb threats, a sample report is provided and useful search procedures are discussed. Drawings support the written instruction that provides the reader with direction in conducting searches. The chapter concludes by explaining the components of a bomb incident plan and cautions protection officers as to the inherent dangers which can result from bomb threats and bombings. Nearly 10% of the threats are real.

Basic Alarm Systems

Today more than ever in the history of security, Protection Officers have had the opportunity to work with electronics and alarms. A non-technical person can easily be intimidated by the term 'electronic'. This chapter will dispel many fears an officer may have in terms of working with modern alarms. The popular term 'user friendly' is a prime consideration by developers of advanced alarm technology.

Alarms are activated for a number of reasons, **least** of which is when an actual intruder is on the premises. This fact is extremely important and must effect officer attitude and performance in terms of personal safety.

Malfunctions are the second most common cause of alarm activation, and human error ranks third in this breakdown of causes. Notable, is the fact that alarms are seldom activated by the perpetration of an intruder.

Malfunctions and human error are by far the most common reason for alarm activation. For this reason, officers frequently tend to become complacent and seldom take adequate precautions when responding to an alarm.

The chapter goes on to explain alarm functions in simple terminology beginning with perimeter protection, and then describing interior protection systems and devices. Monitoring systems, local and central alarm stations are discussed as well as the role of response personnel. Alarm activation, supervision, monitoring and responding are also discussed in this chapter.

Suffice to again emphasize the inherent dangers that may confront the protection officer who does not take alarm responses seriously. Based on 1,796 reported alarms, only 21 were a result of a violation of a facility. While this may seem like a small number of incidents, it is vitally important that the officers assume each alarm has been activated by an illegal act or initiated by an unauthorized person. The officer **must** employ extreme caution in dealing with each and every alarm response.

Fire Prevention & Detection

Of all disasters that face industry today (and in the past), fires are by far the most devastating. Fire Prevention and Detection has always been a major concern for security organizations. In each case when a fire occurs, the protection officer has a very important role. Selecting the correct fire extinguisher, preliminary fire-fighting, activating an alarm, directing professional fire-fighting units, evacuating personnel, and maintaining security conditions during and after a fire are all protection officer responsibilities.

Protection Officers are usually the **the first officer on the scene.** In terms of fire prevention and detection, the officer must make judgement calls that could effect the survival of the entire organization. This chapter gives the reader information that will assist in the identification of a fire hazard and how this hazard can be eliminated. The effects that **Air, Heat & Fuel** have on fire is discussed in detail.

Much of this chapter deals with prevention, which means that the protection officer should be able to recognize a fire hazard, and take appropriate action. Approximately 10 of the most common fire hazards are identified and examples of each are cited. Of the list of hazards, carelessness by employees, visitors and the public heads the list. Good fire prevention practises can be related to effective security because fire prevention patrols can enhance general facility security and safety.

The chapter goes into considerable detail discussing the various kinds of fire extinguishers and their application to fire-fighting and control. Instructions are provided in the use of fire extinguishers and the classifications of fires each extinguisher is designed to combat.

Sprinkler systems, stand-pipes, fire doors and escape routes are discussed. Employee roles in the development of a fire control contingency plan is covered along with the action that will be taken by off-site fire-fighting units.

Hazardous Materials

A lot more attention has been focused on this topic in recent years. The day to day and long term management of these kind of materials is becoming a part of everyday life, particularly in the industrial world. The Protection Officer is now called upon to not only have a good understanding of what constitutes a hazardous material, but what has to be done to ensure that that same substance does not pose a risk to employees and the public. While the types of materials are not discussed in detail, there are numerous suggestions as to how these materials can be identified.

People play a key role in the misuse and abuse of hazardous materials; the Protection Officer plays a key role in enforcing the rules and procedures that are designed to safeguard a contaminated area. Numerous locations and facilities both public and private, industrial, commercial and recreational may be adversely affected by improperly stored, handled or transported hazardous materials. By developing a broad knowledge base about this topic, the Protection Officer can do a great deal to protect people and the environment.

This chapter begins by discussing the response methods to deal with uncontrolled release of hazardous material. The statement "dilution was the solution to pollution" does not necessarily hold true today. Diluted hazardous solutions can have long term devastating effects on the environment. In years past, the job of dealing with these situations was primarily a fire department responsibility. Today specialized hazardous material (HazMat) response teams have been

developed to respond to uncontrolled releases of hazardous substances. This chapter deals with the necessary response needed to deal with the risk of uncontrolled hazardous materials which includes:
- Activate the Contingency Plan
- Identify the substance released
- Determine the quantity of the released substance
- Determine the extent of the damage
- Perform "Site Security"

The chapter provides details of each of the needed steps to manage hazardous materials that are not controlled and pose an immediate threat to life and property.

While each of the five steps are of vital importance, the final step, "site security", is of primary importance to the Protection Officer. This relates to keeping onlookers and bystanders out of the contaminated area. Co-workers, the public and even the media can all pose serious security problems. They must be kept clear of the affected area for their own safety. The HazMat response team have a big job to do and can't be burdened with the task of dealing with unwanted onlookers.

An excellent illustration depicts how the security function can be implemented. It describes the three critical zones: Hot, Warm, and Cold. All non-essential personnel must be kept clear of the contaminated area and restricted to the cold zone area where the Command Post is established and controlled by the Incident Commander.

Once the contamination has been cleaned up or safely controlled (decontaminated or DECONed) the Incident Commander will make a determination about further security measures. Only once the area has been classified as safe will the strict security procedures be relaxed.

UNIT V

Security & Labor Relations

Wild-cat strikes, lawful strikes and lock-outs are frequent occurrences on the labor scene. When any of these conditions are anticipated by management, extensive contingency plans are developed with a view to protecting non-striking employees and the physical aspects of the struck facility. The roles of the Protection Officer in labor disputes include but are not limited to:

- Access Control
- Escorts
- Chain of Command (Security)
- Police Liaison
- Communications
- Pre-strike Vandalism
- Fire Safety
- Building Security
- Security Lighting
- Supply Acquisitions
- Threatening Phone Calls
- Crossing Picket Lines
- Picket Line Surveillance

Other strike conditions that are discussed in this chapter are searches, employee misconduct and dishonesty, employee discipline, types of discipline, arbitration and interviews. It must be remembered that the protection officer's role in matters of labor unrest is one of neutrality. It is important that strikers do not perceive security as an extension of management.

By maintaining a friendly, cooperative attitude, it is possible to reduce much of the friction that is normally present during strike or lock-out conditions. However, disgruntled strikers will resort to numerous tactics designed to intimidate non-striking employees and cause management hardships.

While maintaining good relations is very important, sometimes it is necessary to compel strikers to adhere to company strike policy. In the absence of court injunctions, the employer has all of the legal powers necessary to protect the property and the people having legal access to the facility.

Emergency Planning & Disaster Control

Advanced planning is the key to controlling emergencies and disasters in any workplace. For this reason, such a plan should be a basic part of every safety and accident prevention program.

This chapter presents general guidelines to follow in setting up a disaster control plan, and then provides a step-by-step outline of specific actions to be taken including an organizational chart showing how to assign individual responsibilities for each step in the plan. Prominent in the emergency plan is the protection officer, who once again is often the first officer required to take action.

Some of the man-made or act-of-God disasters discussed in this chapter are:
- Fire
- Explosion
- Civil Disturbance
- Hazardous chemical or gas leaks, and spills
- Earthquake
- Building collapse
- Hurricane
- Tornado
- Flood
- Nuclear holocaust, radiation accident

Once the type of disaster has been identified, it is essential that the correct group(s) or individuals be identified and located to render all possible and necessary assistance. Protection officers must be aware of the signs and effects that will assist in determining the kind of disaster that has occurred.

The next step is to have available a list of personnel and organizations that have been designated to cope with the disaster. Home telephone numbers, as well as alternately designated personnel who are trained to deal with disasters, must be known to the officer so as to limit the time consumed in summoning assistance. Other considerations that involve security personnel are:

- Plant warning & Communication systems
- Transportation
- Medical Services
- Employee Training - first aid, fire fighting & rescue
- Emergency power sources
- Mutual aid programs
- Availability of Facility Plans, maps and diagrams

Security personnel must assume a major responsibility in such crisis conditions. It is essential that each officer carefully studies the Emergency-Disaster plan and understands how his/her responsibilities interface with other designated employees named in the plan. Protecting life and property is a major protection officer concern and it is important to restore full security as quickly as possible. This means gaining control of access points, providing direction to emergency response units and encouraging an atmosphere that will reduce panic.

Terrorism, VIP Protection, Hostage Conditions

This chapter begins by explaining the current state of terrorism. Terrorism is a strategy employing the use or threat of force to achieve political or social objectives. It is a form of coercion designed to manipulate an opponent (government

or private organization). The chapter describes a terrorist as:
- 21 to 40 years old;
- Often female
- Have no criminal record
- Well-educated
- Skilled in military techniques
- Dedicated to a cause

The chapter explains the structure of terrorist groups by geographical location and provides details on the methods of operation employed by the various terrorist groups. Counterterrorist security personnel are given excellent information as to the tactics that are employed by terrorists. Foremost in the terrorist groups is advanced intelligence and careful planning. They will only attempt a mission that they believe has an excellent opportunity to succeed.

Terrorist plans include the manipulation of existing security systems, including the recruitment of personnel from within the organization. They most frequently have inside sources of information that provide them with the ability to strike at a time and a place least expected. Frequently, they will kidnap an employee or employee's family prior to an attack, or they will seize a hostage during the attack.

Prior to the attack, they will embark upon such measures as isolating the facility by eliminating power or communications. They are either experts at detonating explosive devices or they recruit sympathetic groups or individuals to assist in the deployment of explosives. They will rehearse their plan at length and usually implement an attack under adverse weather conditions.

The thrust of this chapter is to point out that effective physical security measures are frequently one of the best means of countering terrorism. The chapter lists more than 25 tactical procedures that can reduce the threat of terrorism.

The author suggests that a well-trained security force, conversant with terrorist tactics and trained in all security areas ranging from physical fitness to recognizing ploys that are utilized by terrorists, is necessary to protect against terrorism.

This chapter also offers readers excellent information on current strategies that may be employed to enhance VIP protection. The matter of hostage-taking is discussed at length, and techniques that are essential to improve the chance of hostage survival are dealt with in considerable detail. Hostage negotiation and release measures are also integral parts of this excellent guide to life-threatening facets of crisis management.

UNIT VI

Human Relations

Understanding human behavior is very necessary for the Protection Officer as duties and responsibilities usually entail ongoing dialogue with fellow employees, client employees, visitors, customers and the public. By applying basic techniques in communication skills, it can be expected that the officer will enjoy a much higher ratio of on-the-job success.

The ability to utilize basic public relation training is not necessarily sufficient; today's officer has to have a better understanding of human behavior. This chapter attempts to explain the underlying causes for certain kinds of behavior. Having the skills to identify behavioral traits exhibited by individuals, gives the officer a much better opportunity to control a situation involving conflict or emotional behavior.

This chapter divides individual behavior into three categories; i.e., **parent, adult & child (P.A.C.)**. These characteristics are described as an ego status that depicts individual behavior that is visible and easy to identify.

People function in one of these three ego states at all times and it is possible to determine which of the three ego postions an individual occupies at any point in time. So, by identifying if the person is behaving like a parent, adult or child, it makes it much easier for the officer to deal with the situation.

For example, 'parent' behavior is derived from the parent or a person in authority. A typical parent response might be, "You will have to be more careful; try to remember your manners". Adult behavior makes the job of protection much easier. Adult responses are practical, impassionate and predictable. A typical adult response might be, "That seems to be a logical solution; why don't we try to make it work". Child behavior is easy to identify; it is basically childish, so you might expect a comment like: "I'm not going to sign that dumb book; leave me alone".

For those officers who would like to make a study of human behavior, you could for example role play to accommodate the behavior of another person and very likely take charge of a situation. For example, the childish response likely is coming from an immature person requiring the take-charge 'parental' reply.

The safe approach in dealing with people, however, is to attempt to bring each individual to the adult ego status. Countering one type of behavior by utilizing another, gets tricky and this chapter is not intended to explore human behavior to such a depth. It does, however, give some fresh ideas about interpersonal skills and how the astute officer can benefit from a fresh approach in the day-to-day dealings with people.

Interviewing Techniques

The Protection Officer has been described a number of times in this manual as 'first officer' on the scene. First officer at a fire, emergency, accident, crime scene, alarm response, a labor dispute — you name it, the officer **must** be there. Interviewing is no exception.

The officer must carefully record initial remarks made by witnesses or suspects, record what occurred at a crime or accident scene, and take statements given under conditions of distress. This is not an easy task because how well this information is obtained and recorded will frequently have a major impact on the action taken by affected parties and individuals.

Readers should review the Field Note and Report Writing chapter in conjunction with this part of the manual.

The basic difference between note taking and interviewing is that the interviewer must take charge of the situation. There are a number of proven methods that will assist the officer in assuming the command position in these circumstances. **There are several stages that should be followed when interviewing, which are:**
- Getting acquainted
- Developing rapport
- Motivating the subject
- Keeping the subject talking
- Listening to what is said

Many times it is not possible to conduct a structured interview, so it is doubly important to carefully record all information that is seen or heard. If the formal interview is conducted by a senior member of the guard force, the preliminary information obtained by the field officer will prove invaluable to the supervisor.

This chapter discusses obstacles that can be encountered in an interview and gives the interviewer helpful tips to avoid losing the lead role. Such tactics as: 'Initially avoiding specific questions', 'Avoiding yes or no answers', 'Not using leading questions', 'Avoiding rapid-fire questions','Not using open-ended questions', 'Allowing a long pause if necessary', 'Not taking the non-direct approach'; are all useful interviewing techniques. The chapter concludes with helpful suggestions on how to successfully conclude the interview.

Stress Management

Stress is not limited to the chief executive officer, the senior vice-president, the corporate security director. Stress effects everyone to varying degrees. It is said that a certain amount of stress is healthy and provides stimulation.

However, stress that is not recognized and managed can have devastating effects — reducing productivity, lowering resistance, causing physical disorders which could lead to drugs, alcohol or even suicide. To lead a healthy professional and personal life, we must have the ability to recognize situations that are personally stressful and master the skill to cope.

This chapter points out that most of our stress is caused by boredom. We have the ability to be extremely productive, but this ability is retarded if we are hampered by the effects and causes of stress. It is not always possible to alter our professional and personal lives.

If for example, the protection officer is bored on the job, there are a number of remedies to this condition. It is possible to create new challenges and enrich one's role in security.

'Job Enlargement' does not mean job enrichment. In protection, the challenge to be professional is a significant one. This chapter tells us the cause, effects and how to cope with stress. It is then up to the individual to create an interesting work environment in an effort to gain more fulfillment from the job. A good supervisor (boss) can often be helpful in making work more interesting, challenging and rewarding.

This chapter describes the characteristics of a healthy personality as:

- A high level of self-esteem
- Action-orientated behavior
- A high level of internal control
- The capability of establishing priorities.

To survive happily in a world of hassles and ensuing stress, the individual must develop coping mechanisms. One needs to start with a healthy personal lifestyle based on values and attitudes that lead to the appropriate use of time management, exercise, sleep, vacations, intimacy and family life.

Relaxation techniques can release enorphin, a powerful natural tranquilizer that can turn off the mechanism that causes stress. We must all recognize that we have limitations and should not set unrealistic goals that are impractical and often impossible to fulfill. We should not actively seek happiness because we may well have already found happiness and don't realize it.

This chapter is one that is thought-provoking and affords readers the opportunity to better understand the complex topic of stress and burn-out. There are a number of intriguing and useful living lessons to be learned and one must read this work very carefully to fully understand how we can benefit from the ability to manage stress, the silent killer.

Crisis Intervention

The personal safety of Protection Officers has to be of paramount importance because each officer working in security today is frequently exposed to conflict orientated situations. Crisis Intervention/Management is a technique of communicating in a non-threatening manner with individual(s) that are behaving in a disruptive or violent manner.

This chapter deals with the causes that lead to disruptive behavior such as illness, injury, emotional problems, substance abuse, stress or anger. To cope with individuals exhibiting these kinds of characteristics, the Protection Officer must develop a plan of action that is designed to reduce the risk, not only to the distraught individual, but employees and of course, the officer.

Each situation must be **evaluated**, that is to say, "what is going on here". Once it has been determined what is actually happening, there has to be a **plan of action.** This deals with ensuring that necessary personnel and other resources are available to manage the situation. Next step is to **implement the plan.** The action taken must be appropriate and designed to sustain the safety of the officer(s) and subject(s). After the appropriate action has been taken, it is necessary to carefully **document** the entire crisis situation. Finally a **review process** must take place that includes all of the personnel involved. This gives everyone the opportunity to openly discuss what happened; it is a positive critiquing exercise.

The writer encourages effective listening techniques. Listening in an emphatic manner tends to reduce anxiety on the part of the subject. By projecting a caring attitude there is a greater opportunity to gain the confidence of the individual. Past prejudices and biases must be put aside and the Protection Officer has to be objective. A person suffering from distress, frustration, anger or dismay can easily detect insincerity. Be genuine and never ignore the principal of the conflict; listen carefully to clarify any messages. Reinforce in the subject's mind what has been said so that he/she knows that you really do understand.

The chapter also deals in some length with non-verbal communications. Almost 85% of messages are conveyed without words, hence it is vitally important to watch for body language that will give clues as to the emotional state of a principal(s) to a conflict. Honor the personal space of the subject and be aware of posture that may be interpreted as threatening. Maintain a position/stance that is non-threatening while rendering maximum personal safety.

The "team approach" is suggested in dealing with crisis situations. It offers more personal safety to other team members, while maintaining a stronger deterrent. Team members do not feel that aggression is directed at them personally, rather at the team. A team should remain small and back-up personnel should avoid the scene unless the situation requires support personnel. Avoid a mass convergency. Pre-incident training is extremely important. Team drills are performed to ensure that each player fully understands his/her role.

In extreme situations of emotional turmoil that has been initiated by an individual(s) that is suffering from severe stress or behaving in a violent manner, the action taken by the first officer on the scene is critical to the successful resolve of the situation. By carefully analyzing the threat, keeping calm, being objective and listening in an empathetic manner, the potentially violent situation can usually be defused. The author cautions all officers to first ensure that there is sufficient back-up personnel before taking a corrective action.

UNIT VII

Security Awareness

This chapter begins by giving the definition of awareness from the Webster Dictionary: "watchful, wary and having or showing realization, perception or knowledge". The challenge is to create awareness or watchfulness in the minds of potential law breakers and a realization that security does exist in the minds of employees and those with lawful access to the facility.

An eight-story building is described as (1) with virtually no security; (2) with a maximum level of security such as adequate fencing — entrance with security officer, CCTV mounted on four corners of the building, security check upon entering the building, signing in and being issued a badge, the party being visited is contacted to verify the visitor, the visitor is escorted to and from the office in question and the attache case is inspected upon departure.

In the first scenario there is no 'presence' of security, but in the second instance there is a 'real presence' of security.

The point is that security awareness must be real, it can't be counterfeit because false security will be discovered and the awareness becomes a negative factor. Effective security awareness must be created through education and the presence of effective security measures that are not only apparent, but capable of deterring illegal acts.

This chapter gives numerous methods of making employees aware of security through a well-prepared and structured education program introduced to the work environment and carefully maintained on a continuous basis. To create a real security environment that is not only effective but serves as an ongoing deterrent, management must attend to the following security procedures:

- Background checks
- New employee orientation
- Security signs and posters
- Paycheck messages
- Communicating security news events
- Videos & films
- Employee information sessions

The chapter describes how these kind of security awareness programs can be communicated to employees through the written and spoken word. Employee involvement in security awareness programs is desirable and can be achieved through the formation of a security committee. Input is needed from employees at all levels of the organization. Soliciting the cooperation of employees is the best way to achieve effective security.

Security Investigations

Most Protection Officers are of the opinion that investigations relate to white-collar crime, involve the mafia with a blonde, trenchcoat and flashy car thrown in for good measure. As the protection officer is an adjunct member of the management team, it is his/her duty to provide management with information.

The officer reports this information after conducting some basic types of investigative activity such as searching, interviews, attending an accident or crime scene, intervening in a conflict situation, or any number of the routine occurrences that involves security on a regular basis.

Generally, the protection officer becomes involved in the preliminary investigation. This is an important facet of the entire investigation process as initial information must be factual, and accurately recorded. Initial investigation steps include:

- Attending to injured persons;
- Detaining suspects known to have committed a crime;
- Finding and questioning witnesses;
- Preserving the crime/accident scene;
- Forwarding information to dispatch;
- Completing a preliminary report.

The chapter goes on to discuss follow-up investigations, auditing, interviews, interrogations, informants, undercover investigations, and testifying in court. The role of the protection officer is often limited to the preliminary investigation, but officers should have an overall understanding of the entire investigative process.

With fewer law enforcement personnel available to private and government organizations and more crime, corporations are becoming more dependent upon professional security personnel to provide organizational protection. An informed officer who understands the entire investigative process is a valuable asset to any security organization.

Employee Dishonesty

Employee theft is not uncommon. In fact, it has been said that the level of controls and the threat of punishment have a direct link to the amount of dishonest behavior that can be expected in an organization.

Preventive security and security awareness programs have a definite relationship to increased loss control resulting from dishonesty in the workplace.

This chapter discusses the WAECUP acronym which is pronounced 'Wake-Up'. The key terms that relate to employee theft in the WAECUP model are:

W - Waste
A - Accident
E - Error
C - Crime
UP - Unethical Practices

Each term in this model is discussed and shows the connection between each portion of the acronym as it relates to losses resulting from a criminal act committed within the organization.

Not all internal (employee) theft is preventable. We will learn in this chapter some ways to minimize, moderate and control criminal activity. This will enhance our ability to be effective Protection Officers. The protection officer can have a significant impact on theft prevention. They can deter and displace theft. When security is tight, thieves look for another place to steal.

Employees will recognize that effective professional security is in place and generally avoid the risk of detection that would precede an illegal act directed against the organization.

This chapter gives tips on observation techniques that enhance effective theft prevention. It explains the importance of effective reports and the correlation between information related to management and increased security. It will provide a number of suggested actions in theft prevention. It also provides the officer with cautionary practises that if followed will reduce the opportunity for unfavorable publicity or even possible lawsuits for acts or omissions on the part of the officer(s). It is essential to understand the protection officer's authority to search and seize. It is also necessary to fully understand company policy and the organization's expectations of security.

Drug Abuse

This chapter is designed to give the Protection Officer a better understanding of drug abuse. Initial information provided relates to the definition of drugs. The traditional drugs such as Marihuana, Cocaine and Heroin are illegal and pose a serious threat to users and employee safety in the workplace.

The term 'substance abuse' is sometimes used to demonstrate that such drugs as caffeine, nicotine and alcohol can also be abused and are definitely habit-forming. Extended use of any drug substance can cause irreparable physical and mental disorders. Drugs both illegal and legal can be harmful particularly if taken in excess or over prolonged periods of time. For the purpose of this chapter, we focus on illegal drug use in the workplace.

This is a very graphic-orientated chapter and provides the reader with numerous helpful illustrations designed to identify the various kinds of illegal drugs. Information is provided as to where illegal drugs are acquired, and how they are administered. Illegal drugs are taken by people from all walks of life.

Of particular interest to the Protection Officer is the user at work. Drugs that are illegally conveyed into the facility pose a serious threat to the user, as well as fellow employees and management. Drug-related accidents are difficult to identify and can have serious consequences. There is no typical drug user/abuser. A drug user may attempt to escape the reality of personal and work life or could be suffering from stress or pressures from a variety of sources.

The risks to the drug abuser are many. Physical and mental disorders are common and these disorders may be of a long-term permanent nature. To appreciate the harmful effects illegal drugs have on an individual, one need only examine some of the startling statistics discussed in this chapter.

The protection officer has a responsibility to recognize illegal drugs, detect the symptoms of an individual under the influence of drugs, and take appropriate action to prevent illegal drug use and abuse in the workplace.

UNIT VIII

Legal Aspects in Security

Protection Officer discretion is the fundamental message that should be derived from this chapter. The law is a complex and changing field and the members of the Security community cannot be expected to be totally conversant with all facets of the administration of justice. It is, however, of vital importance to understand the rights and duties which are exercised in the every-day security role.

This section will examine what law is, the sources of our laws and the difference between some of the more important parts of the legal framework. The powers of the protection officer are examined, including arrest and search. When the term 'arrest' is mentioned, it is essential that cautionary remarks accompany any reference to this aspect of security and the law.

Two types of arrest are covered in this chapter: "Arrest with a Warrant" and "Arrest without a Warrant". Arrests with a warrant are generally a matter for police authorities and the only involvement on the part of security personnel would be a supportive role.

To arrest a person without a warrant is a very serious undertaking which could have far-reaching civil and criminal legal repercussions if complete adherence to the law is not observed. A protection officer who is in lawful possession of real property may arrest a person without a warrant, found committing a criminal offence on or in relation to the property that is being protected.

If it is essential to execute an arrest, there must be absolutely no doubt in the mind of the protection officer that the offence was committed. The officer protecting the property must have found the offence being committed.

Prior to effecting an arrest, every other possible means of detaining the person should be explored. It is inherently dangerous to take away the liberties of a person. Every possible effort should be made to detain the individual on a voluntary basis. An arrest should only be made if there are no other courses of action available and there is a serious threat to life or property.

If every other course of action has been explored and an arrest must be effected, support personnel is the prime consideration. Officer safety and the safety of others is essential.

If a person responsible for committing a criminal offence is arrested, there are several important procedures that are followed. The arrested person(s) must be advised:

- As to the reason for the arrest
- The right to legal counsel
- That the person under arrest is not required to say anything

Once arrested, the protection officer is responsible for the safety of the individual(s). The protection officer has a legal responsibility to deliver the arrested person(s) to a police officer as soon as practically possible.

This chapter provides readers with general information on Common law, Criminal and Civil law, Search authority, Use of force, Evidence, Confessions, and gives the reader an overview of legal aspects in security.

The objective of the section is to help members of the Security community understand the authority that is available to them and how it can be applied to the protection of life and property. The protection officer who understands the nature and extent of their personal authority do the best job for their employer without unnecessary exposure to liability.

Court actions for false arrest and illegal searches can be costly in terms of legal fees and damages if the case is lost. It is the duty of every protection officer to keep current and understand the administration of justice as it relates to security in the particular jurisdiction concerned.

UNIT IX

Health, Fitness & Exercise Prescription

In the preceding eight levels of this manual, it would seem that the Protection Officer is frequently first on the scene. The situations that we have described are very often emergency conditions requiring quick, effective action on the part of the officer. Examine if you will, an officer who has given no thought to personal fitness for many years, and is called upon to react under crisis conditions. The officer will most certainly lack the mental and physical endurance to cope with the emergency. This leads to mistakes and poor judgement which will most certainly compound the problem.

Examine if you will, an officer who pays attention to correct diet and keeps physically fit. When this officer is first on the scene you can expect better performance as a direct result of better physical condition. Good physical condition creates endurance, confidence, self-respect and the ability to make sound judgement calls because of reduced fatigue.

There is no profession that should be more concerned about fitness. Why? Simply because security is protection and to adequately protect life and property, one must be physically capable of performing under adverse conditions.

This does not mean that a protection officer should be skilled in the art of hand-to-hand combat or martial arts — it merely means that the officer must be adequately fit to do the job. This chapter can get the unfit officer on the right track and keep the fit officer on-track.

The first step is to eat sensibly; the next step is to get on a fitness program that can work. Fitness may be nothing more than walking briskly about the facility that the officer is employed to protect, or it may mean joining a team of some sort and getting proper exercise. The important thing is to get involved with a fitness/exercise program that is right for you. Know your limitations and make an attempt to find a fitness program that can be fun or even incorporated with work and family life.

This chapter provides a simple fitness model that is self-explanatory:

F requency
I ntensity
T ime
T ype

In terms of **frequency**, don't get involved in a program that you can't manage because it conflicts with personal and business life. However, the program selected must be continued on a regular basis, at least three times a week for not less than 20 minutes.

Intensity means just that — don't go beyond your realm of capability. Increase intensity over a long period of time. **Time** must be made for exercise, this is the part that knocks most new entrants into fitness out of the program. Don't procrastinate — make time. **Type** is the kind of exercise you choose. It doesn't mean you should necessarily 'pump iron'. Do something you enjoy.

This chapter illustrates some myths about fitness, such as:
- No pain, no gain.
- Go for the burn.
- Exercise turns fat to muscle
- You need extra vitamins when exercising
- Exercise will increase appetite
- Weight lifting makes you muscle-bound
- Protein supplement is needed to build muscles
- Massagers and vibrators get rid of fat

These 'folklores of exercise' are explained in detail, along with all of the facets of fitness that will lead to a healthier, happier life for those who care about themselves. If protection is your career, go for it, what do you have to lose? A fit body relates to a fit mind.

UNIT X

First Aid & C.P.R.

The purpose of first aid is to provide temporary care for the injured with a view to obtaining medical assistance as quickly as possible. The term 'first actions' relates to the following steps that must be taken immediately to increase the life sustainment of the injured party:

- Safety at the Scene
- Triage (identify who requires assistance)
- Responsiveness (level of consciousness)
- Airway
- Respiratory system
- Circulatory system
- Cardiopulmonary Resuscitation (CPR)

Once the life-threatening 'first action' steps have been taken, additional injuries must be dealt with. **Second action** steps that must be taken are:

- Monitoring Vital Signs
- Treatment of Shock
- Treatment of Wounds

The chapter gives the reader **the opportunity** to follow a pattern of sequence of **actions that are designed** to render all possible assistance to **the injured person.** Monitoring signs are extremely important and the first aid administerer should pay close attention to breathing, pulse, skin color, skin temperature, eyes and level of consciousness. Any change in the general condition of the victim can usually be determined by paying close attention to these vital signs.

The qualifed first aider (Protection Officer) must take charge of the situation and portray the image of a professional person capable of attending to all of the needs of the injured person(s). Proper training to a standard is essential, and the first aider must remember that it is imperative to keep up-to-date in first aid and CPR training.

How the public, employees and other affected parties perceive the protection officer administering the first aid is very important. A competent officer who effectively attends to all details, has a major impact on reducing panic, and restoring a calm and stable environment.

The protection officer must understand what conditions need immediate attention. So by doing first things first, the officer will minimize life-threatening conditions. The experienced protection officer is accustomed to being the first person on the scene, and first aid is certainly no exception. Taking charge of the situation is imperative. This can best be achieved by delegating responsibilities such as seeking the assistance of bystanders who can be instructed to attend to such activities as directing traffic, moving curious bystanders, summoning medical assistance, and protecting the injured.

This chapter provides the first aider with a sequence of events that are to be followed in the event of an emergency situation. Briefly, the following steps should be taken:

- Assess the situation
- Control the scene
- Gain access to the injured
- Assess the injuries and treat as required
- Ensure transportation is arranged
- Pertinent details should be recorded
- Prepare any special reports relating to industrial accidents

For the professional Protection Officer, reference should be made to the chapter on "Field Notes and Report Writing". The best action that can be initiated to prevent post-accident legal matters is to properly document as much detail as possible. It is extremely important to solicit information/statements from witnesses. A well-written report will prove very valuable to all parties concerned.

CERTIFIED PROTECTION OFFICER (CPO) PROGRAM
Study Guide

OBJECTIVES

Each chapter in Protection Officer Training Manual contains extensive information that is designed to prepare the Protection Officer for the job. It is essential that the material contained in each chapter be read, understood and can be applied to the job. The Certified Protection Officer program has been designed to ensure that as much security material as possible has been assembled in a one-source text. Certain kinds of specialized security disciplines will require additional study as this program is designed for general security and protection. What a Certified Protection Officer (CPO) should KNOW/UNDERSTAND is clearly identified in this study guide.

ORGANIZATION OF PROGRAM

The CPO program is organized in such a way as to provide candidates with information necessary to perform the duties of a Protection Officer. In addition to carefully studying Protection Officer Training Manual, the students are referred to the following study aids:

- Separate Chapter providing CPO candidates with tips on improving study habits and learning skills
- A Security Quiz of 10 fill-in-the blank(s), multiple choice and true-false questions at the conclusion of each chapter in the study text.
- Audio tape discussing the CPO program
- Discussion questions examining the key parts of each chapter
- An Interim Examination covering each chapter in the manual
- A series of practical exercises and a description of the prime duties and responsibilities that relate to the job.

STUDY RESOURCES

While the CPO program has been designed to be a complete course, there are additional reference texts that can be studied. Four of the more relevant books are:

- Private Security Manual - Kenneth N. Smith and Robert J. Prouse, Carswell, Toronto
- Security Officer Training - Joseph Cohen, Abbott, Langer & Associates, Crete, Illinois
- Security Guard - David Y. Coverston, Security Seminars Press, Ocala, Florida
- Security Officer's Field Training Guide, Lt. Phillip M. Satterfield, Cypress, California

INTERIM ASSESSMENT

Each CPO applicant MUST submit the official Interim Examination. This is an open book test that can be completed without supervision. Each candidate must earn a minimum score of 70% in order to proceed in the program.

FINAL EXAMINATION

Each candidate must earn a score of at least 70% in order to earn the designation Certified Protection Officer (CPO). In addition to fully understanding Protection Officer Training Manual, it is necessary for each student to review and comprehend all of the material contained in this study guide. Do not proceed with the final examination until this objective have been achieved. The CPO final is a closed book examination and must be proctored by an individual that is approved by International Foundation for Protection Officers (IFPO)

THE INDEPENDENT LEARNER

Distant learning requires much self discipline and concentration. The student does not have the advantage of a classroom instructor or classmates that can act as a "sounding-board" during the course of study. While the section in the manual discussing Learning Skills and Study Habits is certainly helpful, the CPO candidate is called upon to learn much, without the help of a permanent instructor. There is, however, some help available. Please note:

A CPO Consultant can be contacted by telephone.
Program Nominators can frequently offer academic assistance.
Supervisors usually have a great deal of experience and training. They can be helpful by providing various forms of assistance and support.
Usually there are other CPO candidates either in the same work environment or general geographical region. Organizing Group/Syndicate study sessions proves very helpful.
Public Libraries can provide solutions to problems encountered during the course. The more research, the more answers.

Distance learning is becoming a reliable, convenient and practical method of education. Many accredited Colleges and Universities now offer external or off-campus degrees. For Security Personnel, often confronted with shift work, isolated worksites and replacement difficulties, Distance Learning is ideal. The most significant advantage is "self-pacing". This provides the CPO candidate with the opportunity to select the most appropriate time and place to study, while maintaining full time employment.

COURSE EVALUATION

Students will be asked to complete a comprehensive questionnaire at the conclusion of the CPO program. Ideas, suggestions and recommendations will serve to further improve and expand the CPO program.

Review/Discussion Questions

History of Private Security   Unit 1, - Chapter 1

1. The earliest evidence of written law appeared in the Code of Hammurabi in about 2000 B.C. Cite several factors that influenced the development of this code.

2. State several kinds of laws that were included in the Old Testament.

3. Discuss the term "Ordeal or Oath" What kind of punishment might be imposed upon accused persons deemed guilty by courts comprised of landowners and Royal Officials?

4. What factors led to the creation of the court of Star Chambers?

5. Explain the conditions that influenced the dramatic growth of Private Security at the end of W.W. ll.

Field Notes, Report Writing   Unit 1, - Chapter 2

1. In Security, the written word is a vital means of communication. Why are report writing skills essential for Security Personnel?

2 Discuss the six essential ingredients of any report and explain why each must be included in a comprehensive written report.

3. Describe how manual and electronic storage of information may be useful to all Security Personnel.

4. Often seemingly insignificant incidents are not reported. How can this situation adversely affect security?

5. If a supervisor does not read your security reports, it has a negative affect on the level of security within the facility. Why?

Observation Skills and Memory   Unit l, - Chapter 3

1. How can effective memory and observation skills improve the quality of written security reports?

2. Outline the five senses that are used in the observation process and how each may be related to the role of the Security Officer.

3. Discuss methods that may be employed to improve our five senses.

4 When completing a written report, the accuracy of a description is vitally important; cite several physical peculiarities that might be listed that will assist the reader in identifying a suspect.

5. Describe some of the facial features that you may note and report when completing a written physical description.

Patrol Techniques   Unit 2, - Chapter 1

1. Outline some of the methods that may be employed by the Security Officer to make patrols more interesting and rewarding.

2. How can well planned patrolling have a positive effect in the prevention of crime?

3. What are some of the steps that a Security Officer may take to prepare for a tour of duty that will include interior and exterior patrolling?

4. Explain the advantages of patrolling on foot and the disadvantages of conducting vehicular patrols.

5. Why is a daylight inspection of a facility important if a Security Officer is assigned to permanent night duties?

Safety & the Protection Officer   Unit 2, - Chapter 2

1. We find that there are a number of similarities in the safety and security process. How can the Security Officer enhance the overall safety of a facility?

2. Explain why effective accident prevention awareness and regular safety inspections have a positive effect on overall employee motivation.

3. Why should management adopt a supportive role in the effort to develop a safe workplace?

4. When a Security Officer detects a safety hazard, it should be reported to his/her supervisor. If this safety hazard is not remedied, how does it affect the morale of the reporting officer?

5. Explain why a Safety Checklist is an important guide for the Security Officer in his/her efforts to enhance the safety of the workplace.

Traffic Control Procedures   Unit 2, - Chapter 3

1. Traffic safety of private property is a major role of the Protection Officer. How can effective security measures be linked to the control point accessed by vehicular traffic?

2. Timid drivers have sometimes been the cause of an accident. What measures can the Traffic Security Officer take to reduce this danger?

3. Discuss the use of a traffic whistle. How can it improve traffic control. Define the meaning of each whistle blast.

4. Explain why a Traffic Security Officer may become impatient and tend to employ poor methods of public relations.

5. Does a radio and flashlight have a role in traffic control? If so, explain.

Crowd Control Management   Unit 2, - Chapter 4

1. Explain some of the causes that result in the formation of the various kinds of crowds.

2. Provide a further explanation as to the reasons certain kinds of crowds may resort to aggressive behavior.

3. Describe the various kinds of crowds that may be expected to gather.

4. Loss of individual identity among members of a crowd frequently occurs. Explain how this condition develops.

5. List three main methods of security force deployment that are utilized to achieve crowd dispersement.

Crime Scene Procedures   Unit 2, - Chapter 5

1. The boundaries of a crime scene must be established. Why is this an important part of protecting evidence?

2. Explain how properly prepared notes, taken at a crime scene, might prove useful in the identification of a suspect(s).

3. List some of the kinds of physical evidence that might be discovered at a crime scene.

4. How would it be possible for a crime to take place without the presence of an actual physical crime scene?

5. The term contamination is often used in relation to a crime scene and the preservation of physical evidence. Discuss how physical evidence might become contaminated.

Physical Security Planning   Unit 3, - Chapter 1

1. How can the Protection Officer play a role in the Security Planning Process?

2. List several important considerations that relate to Physical Security.

3. There are numerous card access systems. Explain the principals of these kinds of electronic controls.

4. Barriers play an important role in the defence of physical property. Discuss the various kinds of barriers that may be implemented to strengthen security.

5. How can an effective lighting system help prevent crime?

Explosive Devices, Bomb Threats   Unit 4, - Chapter 1

1. Explain the necessary components required to construct an explosive device.

2. List a number of standard precautions that must be taken when a suspicious package, believed to be an explosive device, is located in an occupied building.

3. Explain the purpose of a Bomb Threat Plan.

4. Discuss what action the Protection Officer must take upon receiving a Bomb Threat.

5. Outline the sequence of steps that are taken when conducting a room search.

Basic Alarm Systems   Unit 4, - Chapter 2

1. What are some of the responsibilities of the Protection Officer in terms of managing a facility Alarm System?

2. Explain a Local Alarms System and a Central Alarm System.

3. List the various kinds of Alarm Systems.

4. Discuss the principals of a Motion Sensor Alarm System.

5. False alarms pose a serious problem for Protection Personnel, Why?

Fire Prevention and Detection   Unit 4, - Chapter 3

1. Define the role of the Protection Officer in terms of Fire Prevention procedures.

2. What are the three essential components of any fire?

3. Discuss some of the common fire hazards that may be detected in the workplace.

4. List the various classifications of fire and the correct type of extinguisher that would normally be used to combat each kind of fire.

5. Halon Fire Extinguishers differ considerably from other types of Extinguishers. Where is a Halon Extinguisher most commonly used?

Hazardous Materials   Unit 4, - Chapter 4

1. Explain the five steps that must be followed in order to deal with an uncontrolled hazardous spill.

2. How would the protection officer identify hazardous materials in the work place?

3. What is the role of the protection officer in the event of an uncontrolled hazardous spill?

4. Describe in detail each item of protective gear/clothing that is worn by members of the HazMat Response Team.

5. Describe all of the steps that are included in the Preparation/Response/Follow-up process initiated and actioned by the HazMat Response Team.

Strikes, Lockouts, Labor Relations   Unit 5, - Chapter 1

1. In a workplace that is experiencing labor unrest, the level of security may be adversely affected. Explain.

2. Define a Wildcat strike; A Lock-out.

3. What are some of the illegal picket line activities that might be detected during a legal strike?

4. Define the kinds of disciplinary action which may be implemented by the employer when an employee has violated company policy.

5. How can the presence of still or motion cameras be used to deter illegal picket line activities?

Emergency Planning and Disaster Control   Unit 5, - Chapter 2

1. Discuss some of the kinds of "man-created" disasters that may occur.

2. Explain the importance of an Emergency Plan and the information that such a plan must include.

3. Certain kinds of "Acts of God" Disasters are Regional, explain.

4. What is the responsibility of local law enforcement personnel in a post disaster situation?

5. The term Mutual Aid is discussed in the Emergency Plan, what does it mean?

Terrorism and VIP Protection   Unit 5, - Chapter 3

1. If taken hostage, there are several life saving measures that should be taken. Explain.

2. Personal data/information about the hostage is useful to Security Personnel. List some of the data that would be maintained in a confidential profile of a corporate executive.

3. Explain how physical security measures may reduce the threat of a Hostage Taking Incident.

4. Define some of the common characteristics of a modern day terrorist.

5. In relation to Counter-Terrorism Techniques, explain the term, "hardening the target".

Human Relations   Unit 6, - Chapter 1

1. Maslow's Hierarchy of Needs has several levels of different needs. Explain Physiological, Love/Belonging and Self Actualization Needs. Where does each fit in the complete Hierarchy?

2. Several leadership styles have been discussed, explain the terms 'TELL-EM', 'SELL-EM', 'PARTICIPATIVE', 'DELEGATION'.

3. Transactional Analysis is appropriate in terms of identifying and understanding Human Ego States. Briefly identify and discuss the three distinct ego states. What positive and negative behavior might be expected from an individual in the Child Ego State; the Parent Ego State?

4. The optimum life position is of course, "I'm O.K., You're O.K.". There are four life positions that a child adapts. Discuss these four life positions and describe the individual characteristics/traits of each.

5. The ability to exhibit good public relations is perhaps the most important quality of a good Protection Officer. How can developing a better understanding of human behavior have a positive, on-the-job effect on Officer P.R.?

Interviewing Techniques   Unit 6, - Chapter 2

1. List some of the factors that must be taken into account when planning an interview.

2. Why do Yes or No questions tend to limit the capability of the interviewer in terms of gaining useful information?

3. What are some of the adverse effects that result when an interviewer employs Rapid Fire Questioning Techniques during an interview with a witness?

4. When a witness/suspect completes a narrative account of an incident with only occasional guidance from the interviewer, what positive conditions often result?

5. How can the personal prejudices of an interviewer have negative affects on the interview.

Stress Management   Unit 6, - Chapter 3

1. Sometimes there is more job related stress in security work than other professions, Why?

2. What are some of the physical side affects that are associated with a "fight or flight" reaction?

3. Cite some of the more common characteristics that indicate on-the-job "Burn-out" has occurred.

4. Describe the basic difference between our Wants and Needs.

5. To effectively deal with stress the technique of auto-relaxation or deep relaxation have been defined. What are some of the physiological characteristics of these stress combating techniques?

Crisis Intervention   Unit 6, - Chapter 4

1. There are several causes of disruptive behavior, discuss the five major conditions that could trigger violent behavior.

2. Describe the first action a security officer should take when encountering a crisis situation involving an individual behaving in a violent manner.

3. What are the four distinct and identifiable behavior levels that can lead to a crisis development situation.

4. For each behavior level there is a specific security officer response that will maximize the opportunity to defuse the crisis. Explain each response.

5. Explain what is meant by non-verbal communications and how this method of communicating could have positive results in reducing individual violent behavior.

Security Awareness   Unit 7, - Chapter 1

1. Webster's Dictionary defines "awareness" as: 1. Watchful, wary and having or showing realization, perception or knowledge. How do these descriptive terms apply to Security Awareness?

2. Describe several physical security measures that will make employees realize that there is a real presence of security/protection within the facility.

3. Security Signs and Posters promote Security Awareness among employees. Cite several additional awareness practices that can be used to make employees aware of the need for effective security measures within the organization.

4. What effects can "background investigations" have on improved organizational security.

5. Discuss some of the proven methods that are utilized by the Security Department to encourage employee participation and involvement in security awareness programs.

Security Investigations   Unit 7, - Chapter 2

1. Why does a well dressed Protection Officer reflect a positive image before the courts?

2. When testifying in court it is important to be as brief as possible, responding, without unnecessary elaboration, to questions asked. Why?

3. A good investigator is able to develop and maintain confidential sources of information. How can these sources be protected to ensure confidentiality?

4. List some of the conditions that would cause an undercover investigation to take place.

5. A good investigator must have effective personal management skills. List some of the skills that must be applied to the investigation process.

Employee Dishonesty   Unit 7, - Chapter 3

1. There is a direct link between opportunity and theft in the workplace. Explain.

2. Discuss how trash can aid a dishonest employee in perpetrating theft.

3. List some of the ways that a Protection Officer might reduce theft in the workplace.

4. How can marking or permanently identifying company property help reduce theft?

5. Explain how good public relations will have a positive effect in reducing employee theft.

Substance Abuse   Unit 7, - Chapter 4

1. Explain the meaning of a Psychoactive Drug.

2. Cite some of the harmful physical, mental and personal effects that result from prolonged drug abuse.

3. How does group/peer pressure often result in drug use by younger members of society?

4. List four substances that fall under the category; Depressants.

5. Drug abuse in the workplace costs business and industry millions of dollars annually. How does this loss occur?

Legal Aspects of Security   Unit 8, - Chapter 1

1. There are three sources of law. List each.

2. Discuss the principal difference between Criminal and Civil Law.

3. Explain the relationship between Case Law and the term "A Court Must Stand by a Previous Decision".

4. When taking a written or verbal statement from a suspect, what basic rules should be followed to ensure that the confession will be admissible in a court of law?

5. The role of the Protection Officer is prevention, not apprehension, however an occasion may arise when an arrest must be executed. Explain when a Protection Officer, acting on behalf of the owner of property, may arrest a person without a warrant.

Health and Fitness   Unit 9, - Chapter 1

1. Physical Fitness is important for the Protection Officer, Explain.

2. Why is it important to "warm-up" before embarking on a session of physical fitness orientated exercises?

3. List a number of considerations that should be taken into account before one embarks on a regular physical fitness program.

4. The American College of Sports Medicine has developed a safe and desirable weight loss program. Describe their recommendations.

5. Keeping your heart rate in the desired "target zone" is an intricate part of an overall fitness program. Consider your own age and determine your own heart rate during a regular fitness session.

First Aid for Security Officers   Unit 10, - Chapter 1

1. Your first action on the scene is vital to victim survival. Discuss what these actions should be.

2. An unconscious person often suffers from air passage blockage. What is the most significant cause of this kind of blockage? When a person is conscious, what is the most common cause of air passage blockage? How can these conditions be remedied?

3. You come upon a victim who is suffering from a severe arm laceration. He is unconscious, in an obvious state of shock and bleeding profusely from the wound. Keeping in mind the first things first rule, what must be done to save this individual?

4. You are patrolling a resort area and come upon a group of youths standing over an unconscious victim who has just been pulled from the water. There does not seem to be a take charge person in this group. If you were trained in First Aid and CPR, what action would you take?

5. Traffic control on private property is now a major security concern. During regular vehicular patrol you are contacted by dispatch to attend an accident scene. Upon arrival the driver of a delivery truck is found slumped over the steering wheel, unconscious, pale, clammy, cool and has a weak pulse. What steps must be taken to save this person?

PART TWO

PRACTICAL TRAINING EXERCISES

LEARNING OBJECTIVES

NEED TO KNOW INFORMATION

ON-THE-JOB SECURITY PROCEDURES

FINAL STUDY SUGGESTIONS

Certified Protection Officer (CPO) Program

On-Site: Practical Training Exercises, Learning Objectives.

Field Notes, Report Writing
Numerous Security Forms and Documents are utilized during a normal tour of duty. Note daily reports, post orders, log reports, access control forms, daily shift schedules, policy manuals, lost and found reports, site training directives, inventory control forms and other written instructions that relate to the protection of Personnel, Assets and Information. Identify all reports, returns and forms that are encountered during a regular tour of duty. Explain the purpose of each of these forms. Practice the principals of report writing that are outlined in this chapter. Develop an incident report that includes the six essential ingredients of all reports.

Memory and Observations
Improving memory and observation skills is an important facet of security work. This can be achieved through concentration, association and repetition. Identify Assets that are considered to be vital to the facility. Make a written record and complete description of these Assets. Attempt to recall from memory, the location of each Asset and a brief description. You will encounter many Employees, Visitors and Protection Personnel during a normal tour of duty. By applying the methods of memory skill development, record the name of each individual. Prepare a report showing all of the Employees, Visitors, Fellow Officers and Corporate Assets. Practice memorizing this information.

Patrol Techniques
Conduct a thorough patrol of the entire Physical Plant. Make notes during your tour of duty. Practice altering patrol routes. Pay particular attention to security deficiencies or vulnerabilities. Identify exterior and interior boundaries. Determine location of access control systems. Make written notes indicating date time and location of patrols, weather conditions, the location of fire extinguishers, power switches, communication devices, alarm systems, signs, barriers, parking areas, pedestrian routes, fences, lights, hazardous materials, doors, windows, vents, sky lights, fire exits, strange odors, and any conditions that seem unusual. Note any changes in patrol zone.

Safety/Security Considerations
Read facility safety policy. Make complete safety inspection of entire facility. Make written report of passageway obstructions, inadequate exit signs, smoking area violations, unusual odors, obstructions to hydrants, alarm boxes and fire extinguishers, improperly stored flammable liquids, debris on floor/ground, oil spills, slippery surfaces, aisle obstructions, broken handrails, burned out emergency or exit lights, improper panic hardware, violation of traffic/pedestrian regulations, misuse of personal protective equipment and other visible safety hazards. List the major causes of accidents and suggest counter-measures to prevent the common kinds of accidents that occur in the workplace.

Traffic Control
Study local vehicular and pedestrian traffic control procedures. Practice traffic control signals and gestures. Practice use of traffic whistle. Understand and practice use of flashlight. Wear reflective body vests and armlets. Locate all vehicular and pedestrian traffic control signs and electronic controls. Discuss and understand emergency traffic control procedures. Determine kinds of vehicles frequenting facility. Patrol parking lots/structures. Pay particular attention to visibility and illumination. Examine entrance and exit routes. After complete examination of facility, make written recommendations that can improve vehicular and pedestrian traffic safety.

Crowd Management

Understand the various kinds of crowds that can be encountered in security. Relate the effect crowds, riots and disasters may have on the facility, employees and visitors. Imagine how a smooth flow of vehicular and pedestrian traffic will have a positive effect in crowd management. Understand how effective access control measures reduce the opportunities for unruly individuals or groups to gather. Know the role of private protection and police personnel in the dispersal of unlawful gatherings. Practice the various methods that can be employed to control and eliminate crowds. Make regular reference to crowd management planning checklist.

Crime Scenes, Evidence Preservation

Apply the principals of prevention/protection and relate the difference between the method of detection and apprehension of suspects employed by the Police. Establish "mock crime scene". Develop crime scene boundaries, determine methods of protecting evidence, determine what kinds of evidence contamination may occur. Identify those individuals that would be authorized to enter restricted boundaries. Make accurate notes of all crime scene conditions, including names and relevant particulars concerning witnesses, suspects, victim(s) and any other persons that are in and around the area of the crime scene. Assemble all information that has been gathered and complete a written report.

Physical Security

Every facility will require various degrees of physical security. Determine what forms of physical security are in place in the facility. Know how the Security Officer's role interfaces with available preventive security measures such as CCTV, key control system, card access control, security lighting, intrusion detection systems, signs, fencing, locking hardware, safes, vaults, and fire resistant containers. Identify assets that must be protected. Determine how vulnerable each asset is and how important that asset is to the organization. Seek information that will identify the threats or risks to organizational assets. By using the probability/impact of occurrence formula, develop effective physical security measures to counter threats/risks. Identify the first, second and third lines of defence to the facility.

Explosive Devices, Bomb Threat, Search Procedure

Carefully study local facility Bomb Incident Plan and know the role of security personnel in the event of a Bomb Threat. Examine the facility with a view to knowing the physical layout of the facility/plant/building. View all locations that could be used by a perpetrator to conceal an illegal explosive device. Note any items that appear to be out of place that could conceal an explosive device. Know all of the Security Officer Do's and Don'ts in dealing with explosives. Know the components of an explosive device. Determine if any explosive devices/substances are present on the facility. List employees that would be involved in conducting a building search. Conduct practice searches as outlined.

Basic Alarm Systems

Determine what kinds of Alarm Systems are located on the facility/premises that is protected. Once the types of Alarm Systems present have been determined, the Security Officer must learn how to arm and disarm such alarm systems. The danger of false alarms must be determined as well as the negative effects these conditions will have on the security of the facility. Various kinds of alarms systems that are available for interior and exteriors are to be discussed, including magnetic contacts, window bugs, motion sensors, photo cell, ultrasonics, microwave audio sensors and proprietary system or central station. Is the Alarm System transmitted by wire or wireless system, is it ULC rated, who monitors the system and responses when alarm conditions result?

Fire Prevention and Detection

Read and understand facility fire prevention instructions and emergency measures relating to fire detection, containment, and evacuation. Know the various kinds of fire extinguishers and the classification of fires each is designed to combat. Develop complete understanding of the physical plant layout. Know the kind of fire extinguishers available, locations, condition and how they are used. Check to ensure that each extinguisher is charged, properly placed and appropriately marked. Understand the role of security in preliminary fire fighting, activating alarm system, directing professional fire fighting units, location and operation of PA System, evacuating personnel, and maintaining security conditions during post fire conditions. Patrol entire facility and record all possible fire hazards in note book. Understand the components required for a fire to begin.

Hazardous Materials

Conduct a complete survey of the entire facility. Document what goods and materials may be considered to be hazardous as well as their location. In the event of an uncontrolled release of any of these materials, what effect will it have on workers and the environment. Consider the physical security aspects of each location where these kinds of materials are stored. Determine if a HazMat Response Team is in place. What is the role of the Protection Officer in the case of uncontrolled release of hazardous materials. Obtain a copy of the Contingency Plan and develop an understanding of the key players in this plan. Be ready for an emergency.

Strikes, Lock-outs, Labor Relations

Understand the state of Industrial Relations at the facility. Seek information as to past strikes; legal and wildcat, lock-outs and other indications of labor unrest. Relate the role of the Security Officer in labor disputes to organization/facility protection. Know/understand pre-strike plan that includes access control, escorts, chain of command (Security), Police liaison, communications, pre-strike vandalism, fire-safety, building security, security lighting, supply acquisitions, threatening phone calls, crossing picket lines, and picket line surveillance. List the limitations that are imposed upon workers during strike conditions. Determine what legal rights workers have during a strike situation.

Emergency, Disaster Planning

Identify the kinds of disasters that could affect the facility such as fire, explosion, civil disturbance, hazardous chemicals or gas leaks/spills, earthquake, building collapse, hurricane, tornado, flood, nuclear attack, or radiation accident. Seek signs or indicators that any of these kinds of disasters could occur at the facility/organization. Refer to Disaster Plan and determine what emergency procedures would take place should a particular kind of disaster strike the facility. Disaster Emergency Plan must include communications, transportation, medical services, employee training in first aid, fire fighting and rescue, emergency power sources and mutual aid. Carefully study on-site Disaster Plan and make notes that may be useful in the event of an emergency/disaster.

VIP Protection, Hostage Conditions

Identify those in the organization that might be subject to terrorist attack or kidnap. Become familiar with contingency plans that provide for the protection of corporate executives. Understand the various kinds of counter-measures that could be employed to protect the executive. Read and understand the Post Incident Contingency Plan. What is the role of the Security Officer should it become necessary to implement such a plan? What are some of the factors that should be considered in the event of a hostage taking incident. How can a hostage behave so as to improve his/her chances for survival? List at least ten basic Physical Security measures that could be employed to reduce the threat of terrorism and kidnap incidents at or near the facility.

Human Relations
Make written notes concerning principals of good public relations while on the job. Display a positive attitude, know the organization, it's role and purpose as well as key employees. Understand your individual responsibilities. Be aware and observe the needs of employees, visitors, the public, elderly and handicapped persons and minorities. Be helpful to those with visible cultural or language difficulties. Maintain proper dress, decorum and be punctual at all times. Work as a team builder and assist fellow officers when possible. Practice effective verbal, written and non-verbal communications, maintain physical fitness, be involved in professionalism and the learning process. Understand individual ego states and life positions. Observe human behavior in the workplace.

Interview Techniques
Practice principals of good interviewing. Each structured or casual conversation with employees/clients should include the basics of getting acquainted, developing rapport, motivating the subject, keeping the subject talking and listening. Observe principals of "First Officer on the Scene". Upon arrival, record all statements and remarks made by witnesses or suspects. Know how a suspect should be cautioned and be made aware of individual rights under the Charter/Constitution. Practice interviewing techniques. Understand the effects of specific questions, leading questions, open ended questions and questions that can be answered with a yes or no response. Allow for a long pause when necessary. Record the details of a specific conversation that took place during tour of duty.

Stress Management
Understand that Stress is not limited to the senior levels of management and it can affect everyone to varying degrees. Watch for stress indicators when dealing with people on the job. Note stress indicators that are exhibited by others in the workplace. Strive to identify and create an interesting work environment that will provide for job enrichment. Try to develop situations that will make the job more interesting, challenging and rewarding. Start each tour of duty with a healthy outlook based on values and attitudes that lead to the appropriate use of time management, exercise, sleep and harmony in private life. Maintain an adequate level of fitness, paying particular attention to diet. Understand that each Security Officer has limitations and should not set unrealistic goals that are impractical and often impossible to fulfill. Enjoy your work.

Crisis Intervention
A crisis situation can develop at anytime in the security workplace. Consider the five causes of disruptive or violent behavior. Identify employees that work in jobs that are more likely to cause them to encounter person(s) suffering from any of these conditions. Have members of the security force been required to deal with violent behavior in the past? What were the circumstances? Are there any written reports covering these incident(s). Study reports that are available. List support or back-up personnel that could be expected to render assistance in the event crisis intervention action is required on your part.

Security Awareness
Develop a list of factors that can improve Security Awareness among non-security employees through the written/spoken word and non verbal communications. Design a security poster that makes employees aware of the need for effective security measures. Consider employee background checks, new employee orientation, security signs and posters, paycheck messages, security news events, videos, films and employee information sessions. Describe how each security awareness exercise may improve the state of security within the organization. Observe the attitude of non-security and security employees towards security controls/conditions that are practised in the organization. How many kinds of security awareness measures can be noted in the workplace?

Security Investigations
Prepare a security report of a simulated accident scene. Use standard reporting method by incorporating the six main report ingredients, namely: Who, What, Where, When, Why, and How. Include the basic investigation requirements such as; reporting the matter to dispatch and calling for support or back-up personnel. Determine if ambulance, fire department or other emergency services are necessary. Apply First Aid and CPR as required. Record date, time, place and all information gathered at the scene. Determine boundaries of the accident scene. Arrange for complete isolation and protection of the scene to prevent contamination or removal of evidence. Record names etc. of victim(s), witnesses. Interview witnesses to determine cause of the accident.

Managing Employee Honesty
Apply all principals of the WAECUP model to controlling loses to the organization that result from illegal or dishonest acts perpetrated by employees ie: WASTE, ACCIDENT, ERROR, CRIME and UNETHICAL PRACTICES. The role of the Security Officer in relation to employee dishonesty is one of prevention. Identify what organizational assets can be sabotaged, misplaced, damaged or stolen. List the various schemes that are used by employees to commit dishonest acts in the workplace. Illustrate what counter-measures can be employed by security to reduce, prevent or detect such illegal acts. Determine what company policies exist that relate to searches and prosecution. How do these practices/policies influence employee attitudes? Is a search policy in effect? Are dishonest employee prosecuted?

Substance Abuse
The adverse effects of drugs and alcohol in the workplace vary as a result of employee awareness programs, prevention/enforcement methods as well as rehabilitation policies. The substance abuser in the workplace poses a serious safety threat to other employees. List the kind of drugs and other substances that can be found in the facility. Cite the symptoms that will assist in the identification of substance abusers. What is the company policy in respect to pre-employment screening of drug users. What methods are employed to identify substance abusers in the work place? Is company policy in place to deal with these kinds of employees? What can the Security Officer do to prevent substance abuse by employees?

Legal Aspects
The Security Officer must understand the grave danger that exists should employees, customers or the public be subjected to any form of excessive application of criminal law. The powers of the Security Officer in terms of search, seizure, arrest, and use of force must be clearly understood. What is the company policy pertaining to arrests, searches and use of force? Know the alternatives available to the Security Officer that preclude the execution of an arrest or search. The Security Officer must understand the serious legal liabilities that exist in the event excessive force is applied by protection personnel. Take

notes on any situation that could became a legal liability to the proprietors of the facility. Understand the difference between Criminal and Civil Law. Determine corporate policy/attitude regarding Security and the Law.

Health and Fitness

Individual health and fitness are very personal aspects of the Protection Officer and the job. The age, health, past physical activities of the officer, as well as the kind of duties performed are major considerations. For some, embarking upon a vigorous fitness program is not only unnecessary but impractical. Some jobs are structured in such a way that an adequate level of physical fitness exists. This is often the case in security when a good deal of foot patrolling is required. If the job calls for sitting behind a desk for eight hours, that is another matter. Each officer has a responsibility to protect; assess the amount of fitness required to effectively get the job done. Make walking part of the job as there are few better ways to exercise.

First Aid and CPR

Theory is great, but without hands-on practice it is difficult to evaluate the effectiveness of the training. First Aid and CPR courses are available from many sources and it is the individual Protection Officer's responsibility to obtain recognized certification in these vital life saving processes. This can only be achieved by completing a recognized First Aid/CPR course that is conducted by a qualified Instructor(s). All of the information in this chapter provides the Protection Officer with an excellent understanding of First Officer on the accident scene procedures. Every security work place must have complete first aid supplies. Know what items are necessary for the administration of first aid, carefully examine the supplies that are available and learn how to use them. Don't take chances with someone else's life.

Final Study Suggestion

Many successful CPO's have used a "highliter" pen to help guide them through the course. Any information that YOU feel is important should be highlighted. This includes any course material that is not familiar to you. Until you can answer each quiz question at the conclusion of each chapter, address each discussion question and understand how written material can be applied to the job, do not proceed with the interim examination.
GOOD LUCK!

INTERNATIONAL FOUNDATION FOR PROTECTION OFFICERS

CERTIFIED PROTECTION OFFICER
INTERIM EXAMINATION
QUESTIONS

UNIT ONE

HISTORY OF LAW AND SECURITY

1. There is no evidence of any <u>written</u> law until 325 AD.

   True   False

2. The term <u>curia regis</u> means King's Court.

   True   False

3. The Middle Ages outshone any other era in the number of revolutionary and significant advances made in the development of legal concepts which have survived to modern day.

   True   False

4. The military services of the Allied nations in WW II played only a minor role in the development of the private security industry.

   True   False

5. Training of private security personnel, while important, is not the major factor of concern when analyzing the challenges and future of the private security industry.

   True   False

6. The earliest law was:

   (a) written
   (b) passed by word of mouth
   (c) known only to a select few
   (d) both criminal and civil

7. The Norman conquest of England produced very significant developments which impacted on the legal system, including:

   (a) the introduction of feudalism
   (b) the centralization of government
   (c) the reorganization of the church
   (d) all the above

8. The 1600's saw:

   (a) the abolition of the Star Chamber
   (b) the passing of the Habeas Corpus Act
   (c) the beginning of the private police to protect merchants' property
   (d) all the above

9. Police Departments were established in the U.S. cities of New York, Chicago, Philadelphia and Detroit during:

   (a) the 1700's
   (b) the 1800's
   (c) the 1900's
   (d) none of the above

10. The real source and stimulus of the modern private security industry was:

    (a) World War I
    (b) the industrial revolution
    (c) the post-war crime wave & white collar crime
    (d) World War II

FIELD NOTES AND REPORT WRITING

11. An officer may be requested to show his/her notebook, at some point to:

    (a) his previous supervisor
    (b) the courts
    (c) a competitor
    (d) all the above
    (e) none of the above

12. Which of the following should the officer have readily available when writing reports:

    (a) a coffee
    (b) extra forms
    (c) a dictionary
    (d) all the above
    (e) none of the above

13. Security reports could be viewed by;

    (a) a judge
    (b) a defence lawyer
    (c) a security manager
    (d) all the above
    (e) none of the above

14. After reading your daily reports, which individual or group would most likely benefit from the contents:

    (a) the public
    (b) the private justice system
    (c) your fellow officers
    (d) all the above
    (e) none of the above

15. When writing an accurate report, it is imperative to refer to:

    (a) a phone book
    (b) your notes
    (c) previous reports
    (d) all the above
    (e) none of the above

16. Proper notes are the first step in forming a permanent record of events as they occurred.

    True   False

17. Notes are not an essential part of proper report preparation.

    True   False

18. The officer's ability to patrol is judged solely on the basis of his/her notebook.

    True   False

19. Guidelines for the use of the notebook and report writing are basically the same.

    True   False

20. An officer must be able to go back to his notes and be able to determine the best possible suspect.

    True   False

OBSERVATION AND MEMORY

21. The smaller the object the further away the observer will be able to recognize it.

    True   False

22. A person who has distinctive features will be recognized by friends and relatives, under normal conditions of visibility at:

    (a) 75 yards
    (b) 50 yards
    (c) 100 yards
    (d) 125 yards

23. Which substance may kill your sense of smell temporarily:

    (a) gunpowder
    (b) wood smoke
    (c) ether
    (d) electric smoke

24. When we use our senses effectively, we are thinking and being aware.

    True   False

25. Each person's ability to recall information from memory is the same regardless of the amount of practise.

   True   False

26. When patrolling, you should stop occasionally to just listen.

   True   False

27. To help improve your sight you should:

   (a) be aware of what you look at
   (b) insure your vision is in peak condition
   (c) insure you understand the factors which affect your vision
   (d) all the above

28. The position of the observer in relation to the subject can alter the observer's perception of the subject.

   True   False

29. Your sense of touch assists your job in which of the following ways:
    (mark incorrect answer)

   (a) feeling walls or glass for unseen heat
   (b) checking consistency of a substance
   (c) checking mufflers for warmth
   (d) checking the pulse of an accident victim

30. In administering duties which sense would almost never be used:

   (a) touch
   (b) sight
   (c) taste
   (d) smell
   (e) all the above

UNIT TWO

PATROL TECHNIQUES

31. You must know the facility to protect because: (select best answer)

   (a) you improve your ability to escort visitors
   (b) you know the location and whereabouts of V.I.P'.s
   (c) you are able to direct the fire department in an emergency
   (d) personnel, assets and information protection can be maximized

32. A daylight inspection of a facility will give the new security officer the opportunity to make security recommendations to management.

   True   False

33. Detecting criminals is the major security officer responsibility.

   True   False

34. Vandalism can be described as a deliberate attempt to damage property. Effective patrolling will aid in the prevention of such illegal acts.

   True   False

35. If you witness a crime, it is not necessary to seek back-up assistance.

    True   False

36. Investigation of unusual sounds may reveal: (choose the best answer)

    (a) an attempted entry to facility
    (b) movement of unauthorized personnel
    (c) malfunction of machinery
    (d) all the above

37. You should report any unusual odors in a facility as it could indicate leakage or fire.

    True   False

38. When conducting a building check, the following procedures should be followed: (choose the best answer)

    (a) secure door behind you on entering
    (b) start check at lowest floor and work up
    (c) report immediately any unusual incident
    (d) keep in contact with your headquarters or control office
    (e) all the above

39. An advantage of mobile patrols are: (choose best answer)

    (a) coverage of more extensive areas
    (b) more comfortable for guards involved
    (c) able to better observe surroundings
    (d) acts as a better deterrent to general public
    (e) all the above

40. A security officer should seek back-up assistance before approaching a suspect.

    True   False

SAFETY & THE PROTECTION OFFICER

41. Which of the following safety/security conditions should be of concern to the Protection Officer on Patrol: (Mark item out of place)

    (a) boxes blocking exit
    (b) a flaw in computer interfacing
    (c) obstructed CCTV camera lense
    (d) overheating electrical motor

42. Unsafe conditions such as poor housekeeping can be a major contributor to an accident.

    True   False

43. Accident Prevention measures taken by the Protection Officer while on patrol relate to: (mark best answer)

    (a) Taking an active role in Safety Committee meetings
    (b) Monitoring employee behavior
    (c) Noting and reporting safety hazards
    (d) Providing meaningful reports that can be interpreted by top management

44. Employee training has a positive effect in terms of developing on-the-job safety practises.

   True   False

45. Providing direct employee safety training is the responsibility of: (Mark best answer)

   (a) Manager
   (b) Supervisor
   (c) Safety Committee
   (d) Protection Officer

46. Safety meetings are exclusively for the Safety Committee.

   True   False

47. Safety contests with awards are a good way to improve safety practices by employees because:

   (a) This practice resembles a lottery
   (b) This practice gets employees involved with managers
   (c) This practice increases employee safety awareness & motivation
   (d) This practice is proven effective in strengthening union - management relations

48. Safety Posters have been proven to be the best method of conveying employee safety awareness practises.

   True   False

49. The safety committee's investigation of a fatal accident is conducted with a view to: (mark best answer)

   (a) determining if criminal charges are involved
   (b) establishing if there has been any "horse-play" on the part of employees
   (c) determining the cause to prevent future accidents
   (d) find out who is to blame for the mishap

50. Drug abuse in the workplace is the number one cause of accidents

   True   False

TRAFFIC CONTROL

51. A corner position provides a better view of traffic than a center-of-the-intersection position.

   True   False

52. When traffic is congested and motorists desire frequent turns which result in a slow down of traffic flow, they should be:

   (a) stopped
   (b) obliged
   (c) forced to go straight through
   (d) pulled over to give the intersection a chance to clear

53. Proper officer protection against the elements is an important factor in maintaining efficient traffic control.

   True   False

54. Prompt compliance to hand signals is dependent upon the officer's ability to:

   (a) use uniform, clearly defined hand signals
   (b) quickly assess traffic flow needs
   (c) quickly assess congestion problems
   (d) all the above

55. When an emergency vehicle is approaching, you stop:

   (a) all pedestrian traffic
   (b) only vehicles on the street on which the emergency vehicle is approaching
   (c) the emergency vehicle
   (d) all vehicular and pedestrian traffic

56. When directing traffic, priority of movement is determined by the amount of traffic flow in each direction.

   True   False

57. When attempting to attract a motorist's attention with a whistle, give:

   (a) 1 long blast
   (b) 2 long blasts
   (c) 2 short blasts
   (d) 1 short blast

58. The property owner of a private parking lot is responsible for controlling traffic and patrolling the area.

   True   False

59. Traffic control at construction sites is only for the protection of the workers.

   True   False

60. Proper direction of traffic:

   (a) regulates the flow of traffic
   (b) protects pedestrians
   (c) assists emergency vehicles
   (d) all the above

CROWD CONTROL MANAGEMENT/PROCEDURES

61. A crowd may initially exist as a casual or temporary assembly having no cohesiveness.

   True   False

62. It is important that the Protection Officer be able to quickly determine if a gathering may become uncontrollable.

   True   False

63. Members of a crowd that assemble for a sporting event, depend on each other for support and have a unity of purpose.

   True   False

64. Persons joining a crowd tend to accept the ideas of its dominant members without realization or conscious objection.

   True   False

65. An individual can lose self-consciousness and identity in a crowd.

   True   False

66. There is potential for mass discord whenever people gather at:

   (a) athletic events
   (b) parades
   (c) protest rallies
   (d) all the above
   (e) none of the above

67. A Protection Officer in dealing with persons in a crowd situation should:

   (a) use good judgement and discretion
   (b) remain impartial and courteous
   (c) refrain from derogatory remarks
   (d) all the above
   (e) none of the above

68. Emotional reactions resulting in the formation of unruly crowds are often associated with:

   (a) absence of authority
   (b) religious/racial differences
   (c) economic conditions
   (d) all the above
   (e) none of the above

69. A hostile crowd is usually:

   (a) motivated by feelings of hate
   (b) gathered to watch out of interest
   (c) attempting to flee from something it fears
   (d) all the above
   (e) none of the above

70. Psychological causes for crowd formation can be:

   (a) feeling of security
   (b) loss of identity
   (c) release of emotions
   (d) all the above
   (e) none of the above

CRIME SCENE PROCEDURES

71. It is important for the protection officer to summons enough assistance to:

   (a) properly protect the crime scene
   (b) offer advice on correct procedures
   (c) help gather vital evidence
   (d) all the above
   (e) none of the above

72. The reason that the protection officer must quickly attend all crime scenes is:

    (a) to preserve all possible evidence
    (b) to show the client that they are efficient
    (c) to quickly give chase to the culprit
    (d) all the above

73. The moment an officer arrives at a crime scene he/she should consider:

    (a) precautions to ensure personal safety
    (b) injured persons
    (c) notes/information
    (d) all the above
    (e) none of the above

74. Items that should be recorded in the officer's notebook at a crime scene include:

    (a) the date and time of the officer's arrival
    (b) persons present
    (c) date and time of occurrence
    (d) all the above
    (e) none of the above

75. A reconstruction of a crime scene could:

    (a) show the crime was not actually committed
    (b) lead to further evidence
    (c) indicate clues to culprit identity
    (d) all the above
    (e) none of the above

76. The main purpose of collecting evidence is to: (mark best answer)

    (a) enter it as evidence
    (b) aid in the identification and conviction of the accused
    (c) ensure that curious persons do not contaminate it
    (d) all the above
    (e) none of the above

77. Once the boundaries of a crime scene have been established it is less important to keep people away from the area.

    True   False

78. Fellow officers and occupants at the crime scene need not be excluded from the scene once the boundaries have been established.

    True   False

79. Once the area of a crime scene has been established it is not necessary to exceed these boundaries in the search for evidence.

    True   False

80. The Protection Officer is usually the first person to come upon a crime scene.

    True   False

UNIT THREE

PHYSICAL SECURITY SYSTEMS

81. The final step in the process of conducting a security vulnerability analysis is the identification of assets.

    True   False

82. Security lighting is designed solely to detect intruders

    True   False

83. Wired glass is considered to be burglar/vandal resistant.

    True   False

84. Audio sensors are motion sensors.

    True   False

85. Ultrasonic detectors are not recommended for use in an area that may be subjected to air turbulence.

    True   False

86. The optical coded badge can be recognized by:

    (a) its shape
    (b) the solid black bar across the back of the card
    (c) the holes that are punched in the card
    (d) the use of the "bar" code

87. Closed circuit television sequential switchers are highly recommended because:

    (a) they stamp the date and time on each video tape
    (b) they allow for pan and tilt control of cameras
    (c) they allow one monitor to be used with several cameras
    (d) they allow an operator to zoom in for a close-up

88. The minimum recommended gauge for chain link fence fabric is:

    (a) 6 gauge
    (b) 14 gauge
    (c) 9 gauge
    (d) 12 gauge

89. The top overhang of a fence should increase the height of the fence by at least:

    (a) 9 inches
    (b) 12 inches
    (c) 24 inches
    (d) 16 inches

90. Quartz lamps emit a:

   (a) bluish light
   (b) yellow light
   (c) white light
   (d) orange light

UNIT FOUR

BOMB THREATS

91. Knowledge in use and handling of explosives is readily available through book stores and mailorder firms.

   True   False

92. The Bomb Incident Plan (B.I.P.) is a step by step instruction on how to handle an explosive device.

   True   False

93. When searching for hidden explosive devices, open cabinet drawers quickly.

   True   False

94. Time permitting, if an explosive device is found, it should be surrounded with sandbags or mattresses.

   True   False

95. One weapon commonly used by terrorists is hand grenades.

   True   False

96. Most bomb threats are a hoax, but;

   (a) 5-10% are the real thing
   (b) 10 - 20 % are the real thing
   (c) 20 - 30 % are the real thing
   (d) 50 % are the real thing

97. High explosives are usually detonated by a blasting cap, however, explosives can also be detonated by:

   (a) a time safety fuse
   (b) gasoline
   (c) matches
   (d) detonation/priming cord

98. In a non-electric firing system, the activation source would usually be:

   (a) heat or flame
   (b) AC or DC current
   (c) blasting machine
   (d) none of the above

99. When handling a bomb threat on the telephone:

   (a) warn the caller of existing B.I.P.
   (b) hang up, most bomb threats are hoaxs
   (c) keep the caller talking to receive as much information as possible
   (d) tell caller to notify the police

100. If a written threat is received:

 (a) throw it out, most written threats are a hoax
 (b) don't take it lightly, any bomb threat is serious
 (c) save all material along with envelopes or containers
 (d) B & C above

ALARM SYSTEMS

101. Different alarm systems are incompatible and should never become part of an integrated system.

 True   False

102. Laser models of Photo-Electric Cell alarm systems are a very stable alarm sensor.

 True   False

103. When a Photo-Cell Alarm System will not "arm" it is most likely caused by:

 (a) improper installation
 (b) a blockage of the beam
 (c) cut wires
 (d) none of the above

104. An Ultrasonic alarm system:

 (a) detects sound above the range of the human ear
 (b) detects sounds below the range of the human ear
 (c) detects only unusual sounds
 (d) all the above

105. Ultrasonic alarm systems cannot detect air turbulence.

 True   False

106. An Ultrasonic alarm system, utilizing radio frequencies can be used in penetrating walls and ceilings to provide better protection.

 True   False

107. A microwave alarm system can "see" inside a heater to determine if the fan is in motion.

 True   False

108. Infrared sensors:

 (a) are state of the art
 (b) present few false alarms
 (c) can detect fire
 (d) all the above

109. A UL approved alarm

 (a) must be manned at all times
 (b) must meet company standards
 (c) must have direct communication lines
 (d) B & C

110. To properly protect double paneled sliding glass doors it is best to choose a combination of:

   (a) microwave and infrared
   (b) infra-red and window bugs
   (c) window bugs and door contacts
   (d) door contacts and ultrasonic

FIRE PREVENTION

111. Soda acid extinguishers contain:

   (a) a small bottle of acid
   (b) all water
   (c) anti-freeze supply
   (d) carbon dioxide

112. Materials termed fire resistant can sometimes burn if temperatures are extremely high.

   True   False

113. There are two common types of halon extinguishers, they are:

   (a) halon 1110
   (b) halon 1304
   (c) halon 1301
   (d) halon 1211

114. Halon systems are frequently used as a fire eliminating process in computer centers because "Post Fire" damage is less than that caused by other methods of fire extinguishing.

   True   False

115. In the event of a fire that you choose to extinguish, your first ACTION should be:

   (a) activate extinguisher
   (b) direct extinguisher as per instructions
   (c) select the correct extinguisher
   (d) keep exit path clear

116. As soon as you feel that a fire is under control, deactivate extinguisher in case remainder is needed for fresh fire.

   True   False

117. The multi purpose range of a Dry Chemical Extinguisher is:

   (a) 1M to 2M
   (b) 3M to 4.5M
   (c) 5M to 7.5M
   (d) 7M to 9.5M

118. Foam extinguishers eliminate fire by lowering the temperature.

   True   False

119. Sprinkler system failure is usually attributed to:

   (a) prematurely melting solder on sprinkler head
   (b) inadequate supply of CO'2
   (c) human error
   (d) foreign substance

120. Flammable liquid fires can be extinguished by air exclusion.

   True   False

HAZARDOUS MATERIALS

121. The majority of chemicals and other substances considered "hazardous materials" are:

   (a) controlled by national laws
   (b) must be transported improperly
   (c) are not inherently dangerous in their original state
   (d) designed to be out of the reach of children

122. Ultimately, all uncontrolled releases can be traced to:

   (a) equipment failure
   (b) human failure
   (c) improperly followed safety procedures
   (d) lack of hazardous material facilities

123. For decades, the common method of response to a hazardous material release was to:

   (a) notify the local fire department or plant fire brigade
   (b) call the local police department
   (c) wash the contaminated area
   (d) get as much citizen involvement as possible

124. The term "Site Security" refers to:

   (a) sealing off the area pending an investigation of the incident
   (b) keeping onlookers and bystanders out of the contaminated area
   (c) Designating simple entry and exit points
   (d) security that prevents spills

125. The highest area of contamination is called:

   (a) the hot zone
   (b) the contamination reduction zone
   (c) the exclusion zone
   (d) the critical zone

126. Nonessential personnel may be allowed at the command post

   True   False

127. The entire cleanup process must never take more than 8 hours

   True   False

42 Protection Officer Training Manual

128. The first thing that should be done in an uncontrolled hazardous material release is to notify site personnel about the release:

   True   False

129. If victims are in need of medical treatment, they must first be decontaminated:

   True   False

130. The last steps in the follow up of a hazmat incident is to clean the area up:

   True   False

UNIT FIVE

STRIKES, LOCKOUTS & LABOUR RELATIONS

131. One of the primary functions of the protection officer during a strike is picket line surveillance.

   True   False

132. Normally the senior site security supervisor will be responsible for all security shift responsibilities.

   True   False

133. The key to good security in labor disputes is apprehension, not prevention.

   True   False

134. An effective company search program may decrease employee morale.

   True   False

135. A suspension provides the employee an opportunity to think about the infraction(s) committed and whether the employee wishes to continue employment with the company.

   True   False

136. An effective company search program can help a company protect assets by:

   (a) reducing accident rates
   (b) reducing theft
   (c) reducing the use or possession of contraband on property
   (d) all the above
   (e) none of the above

137. Which of the following is not considered a type of discipline in labour relations:

   (a) written warning
   (b) suspension
   (c) layoff
   (d) demotion
   (e) discharge

138. Documentation of illegal activities on the picket line could be useful in the following instances:

   (a) to support criminal charges
   (b) to support company discipline imposed on an employee
   (c) to support or defend against unfair labour practise complaints
   (d) to support obtaining an injunction
   (e) all the above

139. Because of the serious nature of an employee being discharged for cause, which factor is normally not considered.

   (a) seniority with company
   (b) age of employee
   (c) the salary or hourly rate of employee
   (d) marital status of employee
   (e) none of the above

140. The single most important piece of equipment that the protection officer should have with him at the picket line is:

   (a) tape recorder
   (d) binoculars
   (c) note book
   (d) night stick
   (e) none of the above

EMERGENCY PLANNING & DISASTER CONTROL

141. In the event of a disaster the following authorities should become involved as quickly as practically possible. (mark item out of place).

   (a) fire department
   (b) media department
   (c) red cross
   (d) police department

142. To ensure effective implementation of a disaster plan it is important that:
    (mark best answer)

   (a) each department head has authority to activate the plan
   (b) one individual will be responsible
   (c) the disaster team is on call at all times
   (d) the chief executive officer or that individual's assistant is available

143. It is important to exclude government authorities when developing a local facility disaster recovery plan.

   True   False

144. The disaster advisory committee should include key personnel from the fire, safety & security department as well as other department personnel.

   True   False

153. Terrorists will not attack unless they are:

    (a) 50% certain of success
    (b) 75% certain of success
    (c) 95% certain of success
    (d) 100% certain of success

154. Which of the following concepts can we use to prevent and respond to terrorist attacks:

    (a) deter, delay, deny, detect
    (b) deter, delay, diffuse, detect
    (c) deter, decry, deny, detect
    (d) devise, delay, deny, detect

155. "Defense indepth" means:

    (a) having reinforcements
    (b) lines of defense
    (c) defensive tactics
    (d) having a viable chain of command

156. The first stage in physical security planning is:

    (a) assess the threat
    (b) design the system
    (c) implement the system as planned
    (d) evaluate the system

157. Cover is:

    (a) objects which can hide you from bullets
    (b) objects which can shield you from bullets
    (c) the supervision of a fellow officer
    (d) rotation of posts so as to motivate officers

158. Duress codes are:

    (a) secret means of transmitting information
    (b) laser transmitted versions of the morse code
    (c) codes used to authenticate other codes
    (d) codes used in vertical, organizational communication

159. Which of the following is not considered to be a period of lowered security:

    (a) workers off-site
    (b) workers on-site
    (c) rain
    (d) snow

160. Terrorist attacks utilize the elements of:

    (a) speed, surprise and duplicity
    (b) speed, surprise and obstruction
    (c) speed, surprise and diversions
    (d) speed, suprise and deflection

145. When determining which employees should be involved in the development of a disaster advisory committee, the following considerations should be taken into account: (mark item out of place)

   (a) knowledge of facility
   (b) after hours accessibility in the event of an emergency
   (c) ability to exercise good public relations at all times
   (d) length of service with the organization

146. In the event of a disaster it may be necessary to shut down or limit some facility activities because of:(mark item out of place)

   (a) extent of damage to facility
   (b) availability of work force
   (c) extent and effect of adverse media reports
   (d) availability of internal and external protection units

147. The communications of a warning or alarm must be capable of transmitting throughout the entire facility.

   True   False

148. Security personnel should have access to a current list (including resident telephone numbers) of key individuals and organizations that would be involved in the activation of a disaster plan. This list should include:

   (a) corporation department heads
   (b) all employees
   (c) police and fire department
   (d) a & c above

149. Use of the facility public address system should be limited to use by plant protection personnel in the event of an emergency.

   True   False

150. It is important to determine the number of security officers to be required to ensure that: (mark best answer)

   (a) there is sufficient security personnel to direct the police
   (b) there is sufficient plant protection prior to, during and after the disaster
   (c) security personnel can fill in for injured workers
   (d) the disaster plan is administered effectively

V.I.P. PROTECTION, HOSTAGE CONDITIONS

151. Terrorists in North America generally:

   (a) take hostages, hijack airlines and attack police stations
   (b) drive car bombs into secured facilities
   (c) rob banks and plant bombs
   (d) invite mass protests to promote anti-government violence

152. Most common device used by a terrorist group is: (Select best answer)

   (a) radio scanners
   (b) flame throwers
   (c) armored personnel carriers
   (d) radar detectors

UNIT SIX

HUMAN RELATIONS

161. As one progresses in the organization, his/her role tends to diminish in terms of security technical requirements.

    True   False

162. An analysis of human relations skills required of the security officer reveals the following categories that are generic to most situations: (mark item least applicable)

    (a) utilize common sense and discretion
    (b) develop effective dialogue
    (c) work as a team member, be sensitive to others
    (d) be involved in professionalism and the learning process

163. Love and Belonging is the highest order of Maslow's Hierarchy of Needs.

    True   False

164. The Physiological aspect of Maslow's Hierarchy of Needs (lowest order) includes: (mark incorrect item)

    (a) food and drink
    (b) shelter
    (c) sleep and sex
    (d) safety and security

165. The authoritative style of leadership functions best when dealing with a mature kind of individual.

    True   False

166. The methods best employed when implementing a Participative, Democratic style of leadership are: (mark two best answers)

    (a) persuasion
    (b) psychological support
    (c) inspiration, motivation
    (d) authority, discipline

167. One of the premises of Transactional Analysis is that each person decides upon his own life plan, and is not responsible for maintaining or changing it.

    True   False

168. Identify each of the Ego State Reactions to the following situation, ie: Parent (p), Adult a), Child (c). Mark answer key with appropriate abbreviation, (P) (A) or (C).
    "A fellow security officer gets an unexpected promotion"

    (a) "Well, she certainly deserved it, after all, with all those children to feed she will need all the help she can get."

    (b) "Bad news - she got the promotion because she always "sucks-up" to the Chief.

    (c) " I thought I was more qualified, I guess I have not given her enough credit."

169. The life position, I'm OK. - Your Not O.K. results when an infant has cold, non-stroking parents, feels defeated and could be suicidal.

   True   False

170. Psychologists have identified a number of barriers to effective communications: (mark correct answer)

   (a) language, speech difficulties or an inability to convert the message into meaningful dialogue
   (b) distractions because of panic, danger, emotionalism or rage.
   (c) personal bias, prejudice or status
   (d) all the above

INTERVIEWING TECHNIQUES

171. If the Protection Officer is unable to control the interview:

   (a) time will be lost
   (b) facts may be forgotten
   (c) psychological advantage shifts
   (d) all the above

172. An experienced interviewer need not have a game plan when interviewing.

   True   False

173. The success or failure of an interview depends entirely on the skill of the investigator.

   True   False

174. The location of the interview should be chosen by the subject so that he will be more at ease in familiar surroundings.

   True   False

175. In most instances the content of an incident will be covered in more than one conversation.

   True   False

176. Rapid fire questioning techniques will most likely:

   (a) cause the subject to tell the truth
   (b) confuse the subject
   (c) cause the subject to lie
   (d) B & C above

177. By asking a series of questions early in the interview you:

   (a) condition the subject to believe that if you want information you will ask
   (b) lead the subject to believe that everything he tells you has significance
   (c) cause the subject to withold information by putting him on guard
   (d) all the above

178. Obstacles to conversations in an interview are:

   (a) specific questions
   (b) yes and no questions
   (c) use of leading questions
   (d) all the above

179. While getting acquainted with a subject you should:

   (a) be opinionated
   (b) put subject at ease
   (c) be informal
   (d) B & C above

180. Interviewees can be afraid of:

   (a) incriminating themselves
   (b) becoming a witness
   (c) the "uniform"
   (d) all the above

STRESS MANAGEMENT

181. Feelings of defeat, frustration and/or depression activate the adrenal cortex.

   True   False

182. A communications system of nerve cells throughout the body is the sympathetic nervous system.

   True   False

183. Adrenalin and epinephrine are the same hormones.

   True   False

184. During stress the blood thins significantly.

   True   False

185. Sustained and repeated alarms may cause:

   (a) heart problems
   (b) gastrointestinal problems
   (c) susceptibility to disease
   (d) marriage problems
   (e) all the above

186. The burnout process is:

   (a) an excuse for sloppy work
   (b) a socially learned "cop-out"
   (c) a psychiatric weakness
   (d) a recognized stress syndrome
   (e) a common stress reaction

187. Lazarus found a high relationship between depression, exhaustion, anxiety and illness in:

   (a) the number of friends of the opposite sex
   (b) the size of one's bank balance
   (c) the number of children in the family
   (d) the amount of overtime worked
   (e) the number of everyday life hassles

188. Effective coping mechanisms are based on:

   (a) time management
   (b) exercise and sleep
   (c) values and attitudes
   (d) intimacy and family life
   (e) all the above

189. Relaxation techniques are:

   (a) sex drives
   (b) a natural tranquilizer
   (c) evil forces
   (d) inhibitions
   (e) all the above

190. Each of us have spent a life time developing:

   (a) values
   (b) skills
   (c) destructive behaviors
   (d) attitudes
   (e) all the above

CRISIS INTERVENTION

191. Crisis intervention techniques are designed to provide more control of the eventual outcome of a crisis incident:

   True   False

192. Proxemics - refers to how we deliver our words or verbally intervene:

   True   False

193. The objective of any crisis development situation is to defuse the situation while maintaining the safety and welfare of all involved:

   True   False

194. Anger and frustration are a normal reaction of the protection officer after a crisis situation:

   True   False

195. It is better to handle a crisis situation one-on-one, a group would only increase tension:

   True   False

196. During a crisis development situation, there are four distinct and identifyable behavior levels. This list does not include:

   (a) anxiety
   (b) defensive
   (c) disinterest
   (d) anger/frustration

197. During the evaluation stage of management of disruptive behavior, the first thing the protection officer must do is:

   (a) physically restrain the individual
   (b) clear the area of spectators
   (c) implement an action plan
   (d) find out what is going on

198. Personal space is generally defined as:

   (a) 1 1/2 to 3 feet from the individual
   (b) the area dictated by the individual
   (c) the room which is occupied by the individual
   (d) an arms length away

199. Paraverbal communication does not deal with one of the following which is:

   (a) tone
   (b) movement
   (c) rate
   (d) volume

200. When using the team approach to intervention there is a maximum number of team members which is:

   (a) 1
   (b) 5
   (c) 2
   (d) 4

UNIT SEVEN
SECURITY AWARENESS

201. Deterring a potential culprit from violating a facility can best be achieved by: (mark incorrect item)

   (a) creating the impression that there may be a high degree of security
   (b) posting signs indicating security measures are present even if they are not in place
   (c) insuring that there is a strong presence of security personnel in uniform at all times
   (d) making all employees and those with access to a facility aware of the effective security system

202. The visibility of a security program is advisable because:

   (a) it tends to frighten employees
   (b) it provides a strong form of deterrence
   (c) visitors to the facility tell their law breaking friends
   (d) it may well create a better atmosphere of trust

203. There need not be any physical evidence of an effective security program in order to develop security awareness among employees.

    True   False

204. On site physical security components that could be utilized to secure an eight story building could be: (mark item out of place).

    (a) fence
    (b) security consultant
    (c) uniformed security officer
    (d) CCTV

205. An effective security program could require that individuals leaving a privately owned facility allow security personnel to examine the interior of attache cases.

    True   False

206. Increased security measures equate to the likelihood of reduced criminal activity.

    True   False

207. Should a culprit be caught committing a criminal offence on or in relation to the facility, the matter should be: (mark best answer)

    (a) concealed from other employees
    (b) published in the company newsletter
    (c) made known to all employees
    (d) brought to the attention of the guard

208. The security department should make their success discreetly known throughout the facility.

    True   False

209. Prevention is the bottom line to an effective security awareness program.

    True   False

210. Organizational security awareness is best achieved by:

    (a) effective access control
    (b) imposing punishment when necessary
    (c) integrated security systems
    (d) enlightened and informed employees

SECURITY INVESTIGATIONS

211. The first priority when responding to a crime scene is to:

    (a) detain the perpetrator if he/she is still present
    (b) attend to injured person (s)
    (c) preserve physical evidence
    (d) complete a preliminary report

212. The follow-up investigation begins with:

   (a) an examination of the data provided in the preliminary investigation
   (b) an assessment of the crime/accident scene
   (c) initial interviewing of witnesses
   (d) follow-up interviews of witnesses

213. Investigation is best defined as:

   (a) a subjective method used to prepare cases for prosecution
   (b) a subjective process used to discover facts
   (c) an objective process used to discover facts
   (d) an objective method of reporting so that cases may be prosecuted

214. Auditing is best defined as:

   (a) an activity for accountants to be engaged in
   (b) a supervisory evaluation of conditions
   (c) a systematic method of examining financial records
   (d) a check or investigation as to whether or not operations are proceeding as expected

215. Which of the following is not an acceptable audit practise:

   (a) interviewing personnel about procedures
   (b) advising personnel about the results of the audit only when they are subject to disciplinary action
   (c) conducting drills
   (d) observing job behavior or systems

216. Which of the following is an acceptable technique to use during interrogations:

   (a) pointing out inconsistencies in statements
   (b) promising the subject considerations if he/she cooperates
   (c) promising to obtain counsel for the subject if he/she confesses
   (d) placing the subject in a room surrounded by large, armed and oppressive security personnel

217. The success of the follow-up investigation is directly dependent upon:

   (a) the availability of witnesses
   (b) the availability of physical evidence
   (c) the preliminary investigative effort
   (d) the technological resources available to the investigator

218. While behaviour analysis can be used to investigate almost any type of incident, it is most commonly used in the investigation of:

   (a) credit card fraud
   (b) robbery
   (c) bad checks
   (d) embezzlement

219. An important concept in managing investigations is to:

   (a) appropriate budgets
   (b) discipline investigators
   (c) guide the investigation towards conviction of the defendant
   (d) establish objectives

220. When testifing in court, a security officer should:

(a) answer questions with a "yes" or "no"
(b) provide extensive detail on all questions
(c) begin answering questions with "I think"
(d) present a positive image, never admitting that "I don't know"

MANAGING EMPLOYEE HONESTY

221. Which of the following employees steal:

(a) managers
(b) supervisors
(c) line employees
(d) (b) and (c) only
(e) (a), (b) and (c)

222. Waste containers are favorite stash places for employees who steal.

True   False

223. The first step in employee-theft prevention is to learn what can be stolen.

True   False

224. Protection Officers who miss an assigned round are examples of which WAECUP threat.

(a) waste
(b) error
(c) crime

225. It is better to catch employee thieves than to reduce opportunity for theft.

True   False

226. It is important to know who is authorized to take trash outside.

True   False

227. Employee thieves remove company property:

(a) in their own vehicles
(b) in company vehicles
(c) by walking out with it
(d) all the above

228. First observe, then report.

True   False

229. When in doubt about the search policy ask:

(a) any supervisor
(b) any employee
(c) your supervisor
(d) the employee you wish to search

230. A change in workplace environment most likely to raise the potential for employee theft.

   (a) your vacation
   (b) the arrival of new valuable items
   (c) new office set up, (of desks, etc)
   (d) your new uniform

SUBSTANCE ABUSE

231. Invisible psychoactive drugs are completely harmless.

   True   False

232. Psychoactive drugs are also referred to as:

   (a) hallucinogens
   (b) sedative-hypnotics
   (c) mood drugs
   (d) narcotic analgesics

233. Drug abuse only affects 65% of our society.

   True   False

234. In 1982 a Gallop survey indicated a percentage of young people used cannabis because it made them feel part of the group. The percentage is:

   (a) 30%
   (b) 75%
   (c) 60%
   (d) 65%

235. North American boys are generally less likely to be drug users (not including the drug nicotine) than girls.

   True   False

236. L.S.D. and heroin fall under the same drug category.

   True   False

237. Drug abuse prevention is the total responsibility of management.

   True   False

238. One of the key individuals in a counter-drug abuse program is the line supervisor.

   True   False

239. Which drug does not fall under the narcotic drug category.

   (a) heroin
   (b) codeine
   (c) LSD
   (d) opium

240. The risk of acquiring serum hepatitis occurs only when snorting cocaine through a metal tube.

True   False

UNIT EIGHT

LEGAL ASPECTS

241. The purpose of our legal system is to:

(a) set down our obligations to each other
(b) set penalties for breaching these obligations
(c) establish procedures to enforce those obligations
(d) all the above

242. The common law never changes.

True   False

243. The doctrine of case law states that a court must stand by previous decisions.

True   False

244. Statutes are changed:

(a) never
(b) to fill a need in our society
(c) only by a level of government higher than the one that passed the law
(d) whenever there is a change in government

245. The prosecutor's job is to get compensation for the victim.

True   False

246. The police will investigate:

(a) civil matters
(b) criminal matters
(c) whatever they are paid to investigate
(d) all the above

247. A civil action may not commence until the criminal courts are finished.

True   False

248. A warrant to arrest may be executed by:

(a) a private citizen
(b) the police
(c) a security officer
(d) anyone who apprehends the suspect

249. A security officer may arrest anyone that he finds committing an offence on property which he is protecting.

True   False

250. Confessions cannot be admitted in court as evidence if:

   (a) the accused later denies guilt
   (b) it was not in writing
   (c) it was not signed by the accused
   (d) it was not voluntary

UNIT NINE

PHYSICAL FITNESS, EXERCISE PROGRAM

251. Muscular endurance is defined as the maximum tension a muscle can exert when contracted.

   True   False

252. The F.I.T.T. principles:

   (a) stands for frequency, intensity, target & type
   (b) describes the guidelines for setting up an exercise
   (c) should only be used as prescribed by a qualified fitness appraiser
   (d) is only applicable to the cardiovascular component of fitness

253. An aerobic test can be used to determine cardiovascular fitness.

   True   False

254. Flexibility exercises:

   (a) should be integrated into the warm up and cool down phases of an exercise program
   (b) are most effective if ballistic and bobbing techniques are used
   (c) can help prevent muscle injury and soreness
   (d) both (a) and (c) are correct
   (e) all the above

255. Exercising two times per week is the minimum requirement for improving fitness.

   True   False

256. Working above the target heart rate zone is recommended for achieving a higher fitness level.

   True   False

257. Physical fitness is an important component of health.

   True   False

258. Physical activities which can improve cardiovascular fitness:

   (a) are repetitive in nature like calisthenics
   (b) should hurt, which ensures the appropriate intensity level
   (c) should be fun and personal
   (d) requires keeping the heart rate between 160 and 180 beats per minute
   (e) none of the above

259. A proper warm up should:

   (a) get your heart rate in the target zone
   (b) increase blood flow to the muscles which will be working
   (c) be about 75% of your maximum heart rate
   (d) all the above
   (e) none of the above

260. The best exercises for a weight loss program:

   (a) are repetitive and continuous in nature - dynamic
   (b) are low in intensity, long in duration
   (c) do not use gimmicks but encourage lifestyle change
   (d) are not necessarily aerobic in nature
   (e) all the above

UNIT TEN
FIRST AID

261. Putting on splints and bandages are treatments done during the first action.

   True   False

262. A clear airway must be established before artificial respiration can be started.

   True   False

263. When doing C.P.R. it is only necessary to manually circulate the blood for the person who has heart stoppage.

   True   False

264. Brain damage will normally occur within 4 - 6 minutes to a person who has had heart stoppage.

   True   False

265. Two important treatments for shock are keeping the injured person warm and treating the injuries.

   True   False

266. Upon finding an injured person, you wish to do first things first. After insuring there are no hazards to you or the injured person you would then:

   (a) check the casualty for bleeding
   (b) check the casualty's level of consciousness
   (c) check limbs for deformity
   (d) check for possible shock

267. Joints are held tightly in their sockets by:

   (a) ligaments
   (b) cartilage
   (c) muscles
   (d) tendons

268. The proper care for a person with a sucking chest wound includes:

(a) loosely bandage a sterile dressing over the wound
(b) snugly bandage a sterile dressing over the wound
(c) packing a sterile dressing into the wound
(d) sealing the wound with an airtight dressing

269. In case of a person who has fainted, the aim of a first-aider is to:

(a) immediately place the person in a sitting position so that they may breath easier
(b) lay the person down and elevate the lower extremities (legs) if possible
(c) elevate the head and shoulders so as to restrict the blood flow to the brain
(d) give sips of water to build up the body fluids

270. You have a casualty who has an area of their arm burnt, the skin appears red, there are a few blisters and the person experiences pain. This burn is classified as a:

(a) 1st degree
(b) 2nd degree
(c) 3rd degree
(d) 4th degree

PROTECTION OFFICER TRAINING MANUAL QUIZ ANSWERS

HISTORY OF PRIVATE SECURITY

1. Law
2. Sheriff
3. Star Chamber
4. Bobby
5. True
6. True
7. True
8. A
9. A
10. C

OBSERVATION SKILLS & MEMORY

1. Awareness
2. Distance, Size, Illumination
3. Observation
4. True
5. D
6. D
7. True
8. Taste
9. D
10. False

SAFETY AND THE PROTECTION OFFICER

1. Security
2. Accident
3. Policy
4. True
5. False
6. True
7. False
8. B
9. A & C
10. A, B & C

FIELD NOTES & REPORT WRITING

1. Trade
2. Saw, Did, Heard
3. Accuracy and Detail
4. Verify or Confirm
5. D
6. D
7. A
8. True
9. False
10. False

PATROL TECHNIQUES

1. Patrol
2. Fire
3. Security or Alarm
4. D
5. False
6. False
7. D
8. C
9. E
10. False

TRAFFIC CONTROL PROCEDURES

1. Stop
2. Employee I.D., passes authorized vehicles
3. Owner or Owners Delegate
4. B
5. False
6. True
7. True
8. False
9. D
10. Best Answer "A"
    "D" is Acceptable

2 - Manual Quiz Answers

CROWD CONTROL MANAGEMENT

1. Violence
2. Manpower, Backup
3. Remove or Isolate
4. Personnel or Staff
5. True
6. False
7. True
8. E
9. B
10. A

PHYSICAL SECURITY PLANNING

1. Physical Countermeasures
2. Deterrent
3. Force and Attack
4. Signal Transmission or Signal Sounding
5. False
6. False
7. True
8. C
9. A
10. Best Answer "B" "D" is Acceptable

BASIC ALARM SYSTEMS

1. Alarms, Electronics and CCTV
2. Arm and Disarm
3. Door and Window
4. Trap Zones
5. False
6. True
7. False
8. B
9. A
10. C

CRIME SCENE PROCEDURES

1. Actions or Inactions
2. Contaminated or Destroyed
3. Accurate and Complete
4. Physical Evidence
5. D
6. E
7. Best Answer "C" "E" is Acceptable
8. True
9. False
10. True

EXPLOSIVE DEVICES, BOMB THREATS

1. Military
2. Homemade Mixtures
3. Detonator or Cap
4. True
5. C
6. False
7. C
8. False
9. B & C
10. True

FIRE PREVENTION AND DETECTION

1. Security
2. Prevention
3. Smell and Good Vision
4. "D"
5. B, C & D
6. True
7. A
8. False
9. D
10. False

HAZARDOUS MATERIALS

1. Dilution
2. HazMat
3. Quantity
4. Substance
5. False
6. True
7. True
8. B
9. C
10. D

STRIKES, LOCKOUTS, LABOUR RELATIONS

1. Collective
2. Relations
3. Lockout
4. False
5. False
6. C54
7. C
8. D
9. True
10. C

TERRORISM AND VIP PROTECTION

1. Conversation
2. Threats
3. Communication
4. False
5. True
6. False
7. C
8. Best Answer "B" "D" is Acceptable
9. B
10. C

EMERGENCY PLANNING AND DISASTER CONTROL

1. Disaster Planning
2. Planning
3. Emergencies
4. C
5. B
6. A
7. C
8. True
9. False
10. True

HUMAN RELATIONS

1. Self-actualizations
2. Sell-us, Participation and Delegation
3. Authoritarian
4. False
5. C
6. True
7. B
8. False
9. C
10. True

4 - Manual Quiz Answers

INTERVIEW TECHNIQUES

1. Ground
2. Plan
3. Yes and No
4. Limit
5. False
6. False
7. False
8. C
9. D
10. D

CRISIS INTERVENTION

1. Provactive Behavior
2. Control
3. Injury
4. False
5. True
6. True
7. False
8. D - All of the above
9. B - Challenged
10. D - Be sure assistance is enroute

SECURITY AWARENESS

1. State
2. Presence
3. Control, Ownership
4. True
5. True
6. False
7. False
8. C
9. B
10. A

STRESS MANAGEMENT

1. Personal
2. Protect
3. Eustress and Distress
4. Overwork, Boredom
5. False
6. True
7. True
8. B
9. C
10. B

SECURITY INVESTIGATIONS

1. Attorney
2. Evidence
3. Conservative
4. False
5. False
6. True
7. D
8. B
9. A
10. A

Manual Quiz Answers - Page 5

EMPLOYEE DISHONESTY

1. Opportunity
2. Waste, Accident, Error, Crime, Unethical Practice
3. Unusual, Out of Place
4. Junction
5. Reporting
6. True
7. False
8. D
9. False
10. True

THE LEGAL ASPECTS OF SECURITY

1. Authority
2. Employment
3. Employee
4. Hearsay
5. False
6. D
7. False
8. False
9. B
10. B

SUBSTANCE ABUSE

1. Food
2. Infection
3. Nicotine
4. False
5. B
6. False
7. C
8. False
9. C
10. False

HEALTH, FITNESS AND EXERCISE PRESCRIPTION

1. Fat
2. Extrinsic
3. Heart Rate Zone
4. Intensity
5. False
6. False
7. True
8. C
9. E
10. D

6 - Manual Quiz Answers

PROTECTION OFFICER & THE LAW (AMERICAN)

1. C
2. False
3. A
4. False
5. C
6. False
7. B
8. True
9. C
10. True

PROTECTION OFFICER & THE LAW (CANADIAN)

1. Civil
2. Authority
3. Liberty
4. True
5. D
6. True
7. C
8. False
9. B
10 True

FIRST AID

1. First Aid
2. Danger
3. Circulation
4. Strain
5. True
6. False
7. True
8. B
9. C
10. D

COMPUTER SECURITY TEST ONE

1. D
2. B
3. B
4. D
5. True
6. True
7. True
8. False
9. A
10. False

COMPUTER SECURITY TEST TWO

1. False
2. True
3. C
4. A
5. True
6. False
7. True
8. D
9. A
10 True

COMPUTER SECURITY TEST THREE

1. Computer Security
2. Scavenging
3. Carbon Dioxide or Halon
4. Espionage
5. False
6. True
7. True
8. B
9 C
10. C

CERTIFIED PROTECTION OFFICER
INTERIM EXAMINATION
ANSWER KEY

_____   _____
         NAME   DATE

UNIT ONE
1. T ○
   F ○
2. T ○
   F ○
3. T ○
   F ○
4. T ○
   F ○
5. T ○
   F ○
6. A ○
   B ○
   C ○
   D ○
7. A ○
   B ○
   C ○
   D ○
8. A ○
   B ○
   C ○
   D ○
9. A ○
   B ○
   C ○
   D ○
10. A ○
    B ○
    C ○
    D ○

11. A ○
    B ○
    C ○
    D ○
    E ○
12. A ○
    B ○
    C ○
    D ○
    E ○
13. A ○
    B ○
    C ○
    D ○
    E ○
14. A ○
    B ○
    C ○
    D ○
    E ○
15. A ○
    B ○
    C ○
    D ○
    E ○
16. T ○
    F ○
17. T ○
    F ○
18. T ○
    F ○

19. T ○
    F ○
20. T ○
    F ○
21. T ○
    F ○
22. A ○
    B ○
    C ○
    D ○
23. A ○
    B ○
    C ○
    D ○
24. T ○
    F ○
25. T ○
    F ○
26. T ○
    F ○
27. A ○
    B ○
    C ○
    D ○
28. T ○
    F ○
29. A ○
    B ○
    C ○
    D ○

30. A ○
    B ○
    C ○
    D ○
    E ○

UNIT TWO
31. A ○
    B ○
    C ○
    D ○
32. T ○
    F ○
33. T ○
    F ○
34. T ○
    F ○
35. T ○
    F ○
36. A ○
    B ○
    C ○
    D ○
37. T ○
    F ○
38. A ○
    B ○
    C ○
    D ○
    E ○

39. A ○
    B ○
    C ○
    D ○
    E ○
40. T ○
    F ○
41. A ○
    B ○
    C ○
    D ○
42. T ○
    F ○
43. A ○
    B ○
    C ○
    D ○
44. T ○
    F ○
45. A ○
    B ○
    C ○
    D ○
46. T ○
    F ○
47. A ○
    B ○
    C ○
    D ○
48. T ○
    F ○
49. A ○
    B ○
    C ○
    D ○
50. T ○
    F ○
51. T ○
    F ○

52. A ○
    B ○
    C ○
    D ○
53. T ○
    F ○
54. A ○
    B ○
    C ○
    D ○
55. A ○
    B ○
    C ○
    D ○
56. T ○
    F ○
57. A ○
    B ○
    C ○
    D ○
58. T ○
    F ○
59. T ○
    F ○
60. A ○
    B ○
    C ○
    D ○
61. T ○
    F ○
62. T ○
    F ○
63. T ○
    F ○
64. T ○
    F ○
65. T ○
    F ○

66. A ○
    B ○
    C ○
    D ○
    E ○
67. A ○
    B ○
    C ○
    D ○
    E ○
68. A ○
    B ○
    C ○
    D ○
    E ○
69. A ○
    B ○
    C ○
    D ○
    E ○
70. A ○
    B ○
    C ○
    D ○
    E ○
71. A ○
    B ○
    C ○
    D ○
    E ○
72. A ○
    B ○
    C ○
    D ○
73. A ○
    B ○
    C ○
    D ○
    E ○
74. A ○
    B ○
    C ○
    D ○
    E ○

75. A ○
    B ○
    C ○
    D ○
    E ○
76. A ○
    B ○
    C ○
    D ○
    E ○
77. T ○
    F ○
78. T ○
    F ○
79. T ○
    F ○
80. T ○
    F ○

UNIT THREE

81. T ○
    F ○
82. T ○
    F ○
83. T ○
    F ○
84. T ○
    F ○
85. T ○
    F ○
86. A ○
    B ○
    C ○
    D ○
87. A ○
    B ○
    C ○
    D ○

88. A ○
    B ○
    C ○
    D ○

89. A ○
    B ○
    C ○
    D ○

90. A ○
    B ○
    C ○
    D ○

UNIT FOUR

91. T ○
    F ○

92. T ○
    F ○

93. T ○
    F ○

94. T ○
    F ○

95. T ○
    F ○

96. A ○
    B ○
    C ○
    D ○

97. A ○
    B ○
    C ○
    D ○

98. A ○
    B ○
    C ○
    D ○

99. A ○
    B ○
    C ○
    D ○

100. A ○
     B ○
     C ○
     D ○

101. T ○
     F ○

102. T ○
     F ○

103. A ○
     B ○
     C ○
     D ○

104. A ○
     B ○
     C ○
     D ○

105. T ○
     F ○

106. T ○
     F ○

107. T ○
     F ○

108. A ○
     B ○
     C ○
     D ○

109. A ○
     B ○
     C ○
     D ○

110. A ○
     B ○
     C ○
     D ○

111. A ○
     B ○
     C ○
     D ○

112. T ○
     F ○

113. A ○
     B ○
     C ○
     D ○

114. T ○
     F ○

115. A ○
     B ○
     C ○
     D ○

116. T ○
     F ○

117. A ○
     B ○
     C ○
     D ○

118. T ○
     F ○

119. A ○
     B ○
     C ○
     D ○

120. T ○
     F ○

121. A ○
     B ○
     C ○
     D ○

122. A ○
     B ○
     C ○
     D ○

123. A ○
     B ○
     C ○
     D ○

124. A ○
     B ○
     C ○
     D ○

125. A ○
     B ○
     C ○
     D ○

126. T ○
     F ○

127. T ○
     F ○

128. T ○
     F ○

129. T ○
     F ○

130. T ○
     F ○

UNIT FIVE

131. T ○
     F ○

132. T ○
     F ○

133. T ○
     F ○

134. T ○
     F ○

135. T ○
     F ○

136. A ○
     B ○
     C ○
     D ○
     E ○

137. A ○
     B ○
     C ○
     D ○
     E ○

137. A ○
     B ○
     C ○
     D ○
     E ○

138. A ○
B ○
C ○
D ○
E ○

139. A ○
B ○
C ○
D ○
E ○

140. A ○
B ○
C ○
D ○
E ○

141. A ○
B ○
C ○
D ○

142. A ○
B ○
C ○
D ○

143. T ○
F ○

144. T ○
F ○

145. A ○
B ○
C ○
D ○

146. A ○
B ○
C ○
D ○

147. T ○
F ○

148. A ○
B ○
C ○
D ○

149. T ○
F ○

150. A ○
B ○
C ○
D ○

151. A ○
B ○
C ○
D ○

152. A ○
B ○
C ○
D ○

153. A ○
B ○
C ○
D ○

154. A ○
B ○
C ○
D ○

155. A ○
B ○
C ○
D ○

156. A ○
B ○
C ○
D ○

157. A ○
B ○
C ○
D ○

158. A ○
B ○
C ○
D ○

159. A ○
B ○
C ○
D ○

160. A ○
B ○
C ○
D ○

UNIT SIX

161. T ○
F ○

162. A ○
B ○
C ○
D ○

163. T ○
F ○

164. A ○
B ○
C ○
D ○

165. T ○
F ○

166. A ○
B ○
C ○
D ○

167. T ○
F ○

168. A ○
B ○
C ○

169. T ○
F ○

170. A ○
B ○
C ○
D ○

171. A ○
B ○
C ○
D ○

172. T ○
F ○

173. T ○
F ○

174. T ○
F ○

175. T ○
F ○

176. A ○
B ○
C ○
D ○

177. A ○
B ○
C ○
D ○

178. A ○
B ○
C ○
D ○

179. A ○
B ○
C ○
D ○

180. A ○
B ○
C ○
D ○

181. T ○
F ○

182. T ○
F ○

183. T ○
F ○

184. T ○
F ○

185. A ○
B ○
C ○
D ○
E ○

186.	A B C D E	○ ○ ○ ○ ○	197.	A B C D	○ ○ ○ ○	209.	T F	○ ○	220.	A B C D	○ ○ ○ ○
187.	A B C D E	○ ○ ○ ○ ○	198.	A B C D	○ ○ ○ ○	210.	A B C D	○ ○ ○ ○	221.	A B C D E	○ ○ ○ ○ ○
188.	A B C D E	○ ○ ○ ○ ○	199.	A B C D	○ ○ ○ ○	211.	A B C D	○ ○ ○ ○	222.	T F	○ ○
			200.	A B C D	○ ○ ○ ○	212.	A B C D	○ ○ ○ ○	223.	T F	○ ○
189.	A B C D E	○ ○ ○ ○ ○	**UNIT SEVEN**			213.	A B C D	○ ○ ○ ○	224.	A B C	○ ○ ○
			201.	A B C D	○ ○ ○ ○				225.	T F	○ ○
190.	A B C D E	○ ○ ○ ○ ○	202.	A B C D	○ ○ ○ ○	214.	A B C D	○ ○ ○ ○	226.	T F	○ ○
191.	T F	○ ○	203.	T F	○ ○	215.	A B C D	○ ○ ○ ○	227.	A B C D	○ ○ ○ ○
192.	T F	○ ○	204.	A B C D	○ ○ ○ ○	216.	A B C D	○ ○ ○ ○	228.	T F	○ ○
193.	T F	○ ○				217.	A B C D	○ ○ ○ ○	229.	A B C D	○ ○ ○ ○
194.	T F	○ ○	205.	T F	○ ○				230.	A B C D	○ ○ ○ ○
195.	T F	○ ○	206.	T F	○ ○	218.	A B C D	○ ○ ○ ○	231.	T F	○ ○
196.	A B C D	○ ○ ○ ○	207.	A B C D	○ ○ ○ ○	219.	A B C D	○ ○ ○ ○	232.	A B C D	○ ○ ○ ○
			208.	T F	○ ○				233.	T F	○ ○

234. A ○
     B ○
     C ○
     D ○
235. T ○
     F ○
236. T ○
     F ○
237. T ○
     F ○
238. T ○
     F ○
239. A ○
     B ○
     C ○
     D ○
240. T ○
     F ○

UNIT EIGHT

241. A ○
     B ○
     C ○
     D ○
242. T ○
     F ○
243. T ○
     F ○
244. A ○
     B ○
     C ○
     D ○
245. T ○
     F ○
246. A ○
     B ○
     C ○
     D ○
247. T ○
     F ○

248. A ○
     B ○
     C ○
     D ○
249. T ○
     F ○
250. A ○
     B ○
     C ○
     D ○

UNIT NINE

251. T ○
     F ○
252. A ○
     B ○
     C ○
     D ○
253. T ○
     F ○
254. A ○
     B ○
     C ○
     D ○
     E ○
255. T ○
     F ○
256. T ○
     F ○
257. T ○
     F ○
258. A ○
     B ○
     C ○
     D ○
     E ○
259. A ○
     B ○
     C ○
     D ○
     E ○

260. A ○
     B ○
     C ○
     D ○
     E ○

UNIT TEN

261. T ○
     F ○
262. T ○
     F ○
263. T ○
     F ○
264. T ○
     F ○
265. T ○
     F ○
266. A ○
     B ○
     C ○
     D ○
267. A ○
     B ○
     C ○
     D ○
268. A ○
     B ○
     C ○
     D ○
269. A ○
     B ○
     C ○
     D ○
270. A ○
     B ○
     C ○
     D ○